Praise

"*Growth On Purpose* is a refreshing and actionable playbook on future-proofing your leadership for the next generation of business. Claire does a beautiful job tying together story-telling and real-world application as a former executive-level human resources leader. This book is a must-read for any conscious leader looking to lead differently in the future world of work. I highly recommend it!"

> — **Angela Howard, former** CHRO/CPO, Founder and CEO, Call for Culture

"Thought provoking! Claire's clearly defined system for evaluating and growing your business is a great tool for managers and HR professionals alike. Whether you are new to the business world or a long-term business warrior, this model provides an alternative viewpoint on how to inspire your talent to drive toward bigger and better opportunities."

> — **Aimee Therrian**, CHRO, CentroMotion

"Claire Chandler presents a comprehensive framework tailored for human resources and operational leaders. The cohesive and pragmatic methodology serves as a foundational guide for companies. Through Claire's insights, we see the possibility of cultivating a leadership team

rooted in talent and well-prepared to navigate
future challenges."
   — **Wayne Brown**, Principal CEO, Skills 4
      Executives Ltd.

"Claire Chandler brings to life real-world
applications of the 4Ps of culture and her Growth
on Purpose framework for organizations to not
only survive but thrive in times of constant change.
Whether you are a CHRO, a senior leader, or an
entrepreneur looking to scale, there is wisdom in
this book that can be implemented to transform a
company into one that customers go out of their way
to find and where employees are highly engaged and
happily stay."
   — **Natalie Benamou**, CEO, HerPower2, Inc.

"*Growth On Purpose* exceeds its role as a guide for HR
professionals and is, in fact, a vital resource for all
business leaders. Its ease of readability, along with
well-crafted, relevant examples, creates an engaging
learning experience with every turn of the page.
The seamless integration of personal experiences,
coupled with global instances, ensures that this book
resonates on a personal level for all. Reading and
learning along the *Growth On Purpose* journey felt
tailor-made for me."
   — **Christine Asack**, Vice president, HR
      business partnerships, Point32Health

Growth

ON

PURP✦SE

CLAIRE CHANDLER

FOREWORD BY
SCOTT CHRISTOPHER

R^ethink

First published in Great Britain in 2024
by Rethink Press (www.rethinkpress.com)

© Copyright Claire Chandler

Cover image © Shutterstock | Wiktoria Matynia

*This book is dedicated to all purpose-driven leaders
who yearn to do better, to be better, and to make
a bigger impact in the world. I hope this book
motivates you to build organizational cultures
that attract, retain, engage, and advance limitless
talent, so you can pursue — and achieve — perpetual
Growth On Purpose. Your journey starts here.*

Contents

Foreword   1

Introduction   5

1   The Drivers Of Business Value   15

How to value your business   17

Why culture matters   20

How to measure culture   22

The role of HR   26

The 4Ps   27

How to activate the 4Ps... and what *not* to do   32

Key takeaways   34

Time to apply   35

2   How To Grow Your Business... On Purpose   37

What it means to grow on purpose   38

The Growth on Purpose model   40

The payoffs of Growth on Purpose   45

Key takeaways   47

Time to apply   48

3 Aspiration   49

Clarity and stability   50

The "before" state: Low attraction   52

The Aspiration pillar   53

What Aspiration looks like   60

The "ideal" state: Magnetic purpose   65

Powerful questions   66

Key takeaways   67

Time to apply   68

4 Awareness Of Self   71

Feeding your passion   72

The "before" state: Low retention   73

The Awareness pillar   77

What Awareness looks like   82

The "ideal" state: Limitless talent   86

Powerful questions   87

Key takeaways   88

Time to apply   89

5 Acceleration Of Trust   **91**

Trust is hard to win and easy to lose   92

The "before" state: Low engagement   94

The Acceleration pillar   98

What Acceleration looks like   101

The "ideal" state: Cultural cohesion   109

Powerful questions   110

Key takeaways   111

Time to apply   112

6 Alignment On What Matters   **115**

Powerful connections   116

The "before" state: Low IHR   118

The Alignment pillar   123

What Alignment looks like   126

The "ideal" state: Strategic fulfillment   138

Powerful questions   139

Key takeaways   140

Time to apply   141

7 Time To Grow   **145**

Culture matters: Measure it, then move it   146

The four pillars   148

The right components in the right order   151

The result   153

What next?   155

Key takeaways   159

Time to apply   159

Conclusion   **161**

Final Thoughts   **165**

References   **169**

Acknowledgements   **175**

Other Books by Claire Chandler   **177**

The Author   **179**

Foreword

Culture matters. It is said that culture eats strategy for breakfast. Personally, I prefer Pop Tarts and a bowl of Wheaties, but unless culture starts eating strategy for lunch, dinner, and between-meal snacks, we pretty much let culture do its thing.

Employees no longer feel the need to do what they're told. They have options. They can go where they feel they belong—or, rather, where they feel they're needed. When employees find the right culture, they stay longer, they contribute at deeper levels, they solve bigger problems, and they help their companies smash their growth expectations.

Like I said: culture matters.

That's what *Growth On Purpose* is all about: how to create a culture that attracts the right talent like a magnet, then nurture that talent so it helps you fulfill your organizational purpose.

I first met Claire Chandler almost 20 years ago, when she was still fighting to strengthen organizational cultures from inside the walls of corporate America. Since then, I have witnessed her break out of her corporate shell and into her entrepreneurial calling. She has dedicated her life's work to ending workplace misery by transforming leaders one organization at a time.

For as long as I have known Claire, she has passionately believed that culture matters, and that the biggest impact on the culture of a company is its leaders. That's why we have both built our businesses around the purpose of helping them do better. Helping them *be* better.

But they just keep getting in their own way. They're fighting like spawning salmon against the roaring rapids of weak brand reputation, high turnover, low trust, and leaky talent pipelines.

(Drip. Drip.)

You hear that?

This book will help you and your organization get *out* of your own way. It walks you through Claire's unique methodology for fueling perpetual growth by building your business on four strong pillars (the 4As):

1. Aspiration, which attracts the right talent through a magnetic purpose;

2. Awareness, which retains talent by putting them in the best position to succeed;

3. Acceleration, which engages talent in solving your biggest problems; and

4. Alignment, which advances both *their* careers and *your* growth strategy.

This book destroys your long-held assumption that people are interchangeable, being a leader is difficult, and achieving sustainable business growth is impossible.

Seriously, friends. This is not rocket science. And you're not a NASA engineer. Once you read Claire's book, you will have that head-slapping epiphany that you've been overcomplicating this "managing growth" thing. Likely for years.

It's time to apply Claire's simple, straightforward approach to attracting, retaining, engaging, and advancing the right talent toward fulfillment of your shared purpose. When you seed your business with the right talent, and you nurture them through the 4As, you will fuel perpetual growth.

Or... you can keep doing business the way you're doing it today. It's your call.

No more doomscrolling through your news feed and your email inbox. Invest in your business by reading this book. Right now. Before another one of your top talent finds the exit. (Drip. Drip.)

Read up, and get out of your own way.

Scott Christopher
President, Levity Matters; best-selling author of *The Levity Effect*, *People People*, and *The Seven UPs of Happiness*; part-time Hollywood E-Lister;
www.levitymatters.com

Introduction

Leadership Principle 1:
Leaders own their walk

The year was 2010. I was the vice president of human resources for a large global company. I was traveling three weeks out of every four, leading a highly talented team, and steadily climbing the corporate ladder.

One day, my boss stopped me as I walked down the hall.

"You need to tone down your walk," he said.

"Um… what?" was my eloquent reply.

"Your walk," he explained. "It's too bouncy. Too happy. People will think you're up to something, like you know something they don't."

Armed with that sage advice, I returned to my office.

Spoiler alert: I did not tone down my walk. But I also didn't realize, in that moment, how close I was to leaving my job. Or that I could choose to do so... and walk toward something better.

I felt trapped. Trapped in a "secure," high-paying job, on an executive track, within an organization that wanted me to suppress my unique personality to continue to ascend. At the time, I was convinced that this was just how work was supposed to be. After all, as the memes remind us, "If we were supposed to enjoy it, it wouldn't be called work."

Most corporate cultures are rife with stories like mine: Stories emblematic of corporate cultures that say they want people with entrepreneurial spirit to join their team, but instead require—and reward—compliance and conformity.

Thinking back to this brief interaction with my boss, I can confidently draw two conclusions:

1. While he had an executive title, he was *not* a leader.

2. Since you've picked up this book, you don't want to be that guy.

As a leader, you need to be many things:

- Visionary, yet grounded; strategic, yet tactical; both a coach and a connector; both business-savvy and people-centric.

- Politically astute enough to build and maintain positive relationships with the board. Market-savvy enough to outthink your competition. Self-aware enough to communicate the mission, the vision, and the message with authenticity, transparency, and personal conviction.

- Able to keep the organizational pond fully stocked with the right talent, to ensure that high turnover, low engagement, and succession gaps do not prevent the business from fulfilling its growth strategy.

It's enough to make you *not* want to be a leader. Oh, but when it works…

- When you envision a future for your business that your people can't wait to help you realize

- When you put the right people in the right roles to deliver engaged, exceptional performance

- When you have a strong, positive culture that amplifies growth

- When you have a talent pipeline that nourishes itself

...you can truly, easily, and sustainably grow on purpose.

This book is designed to help you drive growth on purpose. It walks you through the proven frameworks and principles that any leader, at any stage of their career, can apply to improve the culture, engagement, and retention within their business.

In this book, you will discover:

- The four telltale signs that your growth strategy is vulnerable

- How the 4Ps of culture work together to fortify that growth strategy

- The four pillars of the Growth on Purpose model and how to apply them quickly and easily to your business

- How to build a talent ecosystem that attracts, retains, engages, and mobilizes the right talent to fuel your perpetual growth

- The tangible and sustainable payoffs of the Growth on Purpose model

- How your leadership role positions you to drive growth, nurture talent, and ensure your legacy

This book is for you if you want to transform your workforce and the way your organization values and invests in talent, so you can drive tangible, measurable business value. If you want to create a legacy that outlasts your tenure. And if you want to progress to an even bigger, more impactful leadership role.

I'm both a corporate survivor and a cancer survivor. In fact, it was the cancer diagnosis I received in 2011 that inspired me to walk away from my corporate job and form my executive advisory business. Today, my clients are executive leaders of growing organizations who struggle with the high pressure and deep isolation that come with their role. I specialize in helping them unlock the limitless talent, build the cultural cohesion, and ignite the strategic fulfillment necessary for their organizations to grow on purpose.

This book presents my breakthrough Growth on Purpose model for expanding your business without losing your best talent. It's a model based on clearly defining your long-term vision, removing the barriers to creating limitless talent, forming teams that solve your greatest challenges, and bulletproofing the path to fulfilling your business strategy. It includes industry research, case studies, and personal stories that bring each pillar to life, and shows you how to apply these to your unique business. It also provides a blueprint for aligning your talent strategy with your business strategy, and for inspiring your CEO and your board to make the necessary investments in your talent plan.

The principles in this book have been applied across multiple industries. Leaders who implement this model have quadrupled their employee engagement rates, increased their revenue six-fold, maximized their profitability, and/or doubled their market presence.

I believe so strongly in this model that "Grow on Purpose" is one of the core values of my business.

Throughout this book, I will share my guiding principles for every leader.

The first principle, inspired by my less than inspiring exchange with my then-boss, is: "Leaders own their walk." Rather than toning down your walk and advising your people to do the same, I challenge you to lead with authenticity. Stop regarding your leadership position as a role you play, and embrace it as an obligation to live, work, and lead with your unique personality on full display.

True leaders don't emulate other leaders; they are deeply self-aware and beautifully flawed, and they step into their strengths with vulnerability, transparency, and personal accountability. When you do that—when you own your walk—your people will follow you willingly and enthusiastically.

If you've read any of Brené Brown's brilliant work on the power of vulnerability, such as *Dare To Lead*, you know that embracing your unique personality and the personalities of your people, instead of suppressing your humanness and vulnerability, is mission-critical.

Leaders shape cultures, and culture drives success. That's why my purpose is to end workplace misery by helping the right leaders bring together the right talent into the right culture to achieve the biggest "why" they can imagine.

Here's the truth: Most of your people do *not* want to leave your company and leap into the entrepreneurial unknown. But you're not making it easy for them to stay with you. They want to feel driven, not trapped. They want to be led, not manipulated.

Be *that* kind of leader. Build *that* kind of culture. Learn to *grow on purpose*.

I want to help create a world where everyone loves their work, feels a tangible connection between what they do and why it matters, and contributes their best talent, ideas, and energies to fulfilling organizational missions that truly move and inspire others.

Consider this your invitation to join the Growth on Purpose journey. On it, you will create a stronger culture that amplifies growth, build a talent pipeline that nourishes itself, and attract and retain more of the right people to fulfill your mission. If you've been waiting for the right time to begin that journey, this is it. This book is designed to help you seize that opportunity. I've got you.

Throughout this book, we'll explore how leadership principles and practices apply to everything from deep outer space exploration to the inner workings of the National Football League. I'll also share case studies adapted from actual situations of real leaders in companies that are applying the Growth on Purpose model to create sustainable growth. Some of the details have been changed to protect my clients' confidentiality.

It's important to understand something about these client stories: I don't get these results; *they* do. My role in their success is to share best practices, draw insights, and make connections between the strengths they already possess and the best ways to play to those strengths.

The Growth on Purpose framework can do that for you too. It meets you and your business where you are, helps you to deeply understand what drives you, and pinpoints the exact moves you need to make to walk the path toward perpetual growth.

We will dive deep into the framework and its application. At the end of each section, there are several questions for you to reflect on, and then actions to apply what you're learning. You may need to read this book multiple times to absorb the strategies and tactics and determine how best to incorporate them into your business, so be prepared to take lots of notes.

This book will guide you toward being a greater leader, shaping a stronger culture, and building a world-impacting company. When you're ready to own your walk and grow your business on purpose, turn the page and let's get started.

ONE

The Drivers Of Business Value

The forces that drive business value have changed, and they've changed for good. We now live in an intellectual economy, in a dramatic shift from the industrial economy that shaped organizations as recently as thirty years ago. The "command and control" style that was the go-to leadership method in the industrial economy, referenced by Robert Glazer in "'Command and Control' Leadership Is Dead", was shaped by the leaders of the time, most of whom had transitioned from military leadership positions.

In the intellectual economy, that leadership style doesn't fly. The employees who will join your ranks, stay long enough to make an impact, and contribute their whole heads, hands, and hearts to fulfilling your organizational purpose want to feel seen, heard, and understood. They want to be recognized for their contributions. They want to feel included in the decision-making. And they want to belong to a mission-driven community that enables them to make a bigger impact than they could make alone. Add the Covid-19 pandemic to the mix, and that need for community is now reinforced by a globally shared experience that forever shifted our perspective from "living to work" to "preserving my health and wellbeing."

To attract and retain top talent in today's intellectual economy, leaders need to adopt a new style of leadership—one based on trust, collaboration, and empowerment. You need to create a safe and supportive environment where employees feel comfortable sharing their ideas, taking risks, and failing forward. You need to delegate effectively and give employees the autonomy they need to do their best work. You need to trust your people, and they need to trust you.

The leaders who can make this shift will be the ones who succeed in the intellectual economy. They will be able to build a high-performing workforce that is committed to working together to fulfill your organization's purpose.

This chapter explores the drivers of change in the intellectual economy and the implications for leadership. It also provides practical advice on how leaders can adapt their style to meet the needs of the twenty-first century workforce.

Leadership Principle 2: Leaders shape culture

The greatest impact on the culture of a company—by far—is the behavior of its leaders. And as myriad business leaders and management consultants—including writer and psychologist Peter Drucker, former Ford CEO Mark Fields, and former Merck CEO Richard Clark—have espoused, as cited by Michael Reidy, when your culture and your strategy are misaligned, culture eclipses strategy every time. Culture forms the foundation of your business. It's not a "nice to have"; it's mission-critical. Ignore your culture and your company will implode. It's that simple.

Since you can't improve what you don't measure, let's dig into how to measure the true value of your business, so you can build the culture that drives perpetual growth.

How to value your business

Do a Google search on "how to calculate business value" and you'll get dozens if not hundreds of formulas. But in the simplest of terms:

$$Business\ Value = Profit \times Multiple$$

The profit side of the equation is fairly straightforward. It's fixed, finite, and predominantly impacted by your tangible assets—your technology, products, operations, and financial capital.

The multiple side is more interesting because it's far more dynamic. It's wildly variable, potentially limitless, and primarily driven by your intangible assets—your brand, services, intellectual property and institutional knowledge, and *human* capital. Talk about wildcards. But when leveraged correctly, it's the wildcards that are the key to growth.

Over the last three decades, we have seen a profound shift in what drives business value. Aswath Damodaran, renowned professor of corporate finance and valuation at the Stern School of Business at New York University, has charted this shift from an industrial economy that is dependent on the output of physical machinery or capital, to an intellectual economy that is primarily dependent on the output of the human mind. In the earlier industrial economy, up to 95% of the value of a business was driven by tangible assets, such as technology, products, operations, and financial capital. In today's intellectual economy, nearly 75% of business value is driven by intangible assets: a company's brand, services, knowledge, and human capital.

This presents a problem, since intangible assets can't be measured. Right?

Wrong. Not only can intangible assets be measured, but you *must* measure them to have any chance of growing on purpose.

Your multiplier

Let's return to our business value equation:

$$\text{Business Value} = \text{Profit} \times \text{Multiple}$$

When you focus on profit, the math is simple: Revenue up, expenses down. But the multiple is where the magic happens. Several things determine what that multiple is:

- The quality of your people (your talent)
- The capacity, capability, and cohesion of your leaders
- The alignment of your culture with your strategy

"Culture" is the key word. Culture is foundational. And, contrary to the myth that culture forms organically or bubbles up from the front lines of your company, the truth is that leaders shape culture. And culture drives success. Culture is the real multiplier of value in your business.

AON Hewitt found that seven of the top ten drivers of failure in mergers and acquisitions (M&A) are related to culture. They include drivers such as:

- Cultural integration issues
- Inconsistent or unclear communication of synergy objectives

- Insufficient attention to people issues

- Leadership infighting

- Inappropriate organizational structure

Sound familiar? Whether your organization is growing through M&A, expansion into new geographies or lines of business, or the addition of one new hire at a time, these drivers can propel or destroy your business.

Let's play this out. The longer you ignore culture—or at least don't actively nurture it—the more you will run into problems that will only get progressively worse, such as:

- Poorer individual and team performance

- Lower market competitiveness

- Less innovation and growth, leading to stagnation and potentially the death of your business

As the saying goes, let's "Kill the monster while it's small," and solve these problems as soon as possible.

Why culture matters

The late, great Tony Hsieh, former CEO of Zappos, not only knew what a strong, fit culture looked like—he and his team documented it. The *Zappos Culture Book*, published annually, serves as a written testimonial of the organizational culture of Zappos, as defined by its employees, customers, and partners.

Years ago, I had the honor of meeting Tony after he spoke at a national HR conference. I learned that every new hire at Zappos—regardless of position or level—spent their first two weeks of employment working in their Arkansas-based customer service center, so that they understood what Zappos was all about: Delivering happiness. This model paid dividends—not only in terms of the financial performance of the company, but in the culture that every employee was empowered to contribute to and nurture.

Tony shared a story that has stayed with me to this day. A man had called Zappos' customer service and was clearly upset. His wife had ordered a pair of shoes, but she had unexpectedly passed away before they arrived. Overcome with emotion, the man said to the customer service representative, "I don't know what to do with these shoes." What the representative did *not* say was, "Let me place you on a brief hold while I find someone better qualified to deal with this." Not even close. Since every member of the Zappos culture was empowered to deliver happiness, she knew exactly what to do. She expressed genuine sympathy, and then said, "I don't want you to give these shoes another thought. Simply return them and we will refund your money." But she didn't stop there.

She then sent flowers to the man on behalf of Zappos. The customer service representative didn't have to get her manager's approval; she took immediate action because she knew the right thing to do, and she was empowered to do it.

Do all of your employees know the right thing to do? Do you intentionally onboard, develop, recognize, and reward them for living your values and strengthening your culture? Do you empower them to address challenges at the earliest point of impact? Customer service is one of the hardest jobs in any business. It's even harder if those who occupy these roles don't see a connection between how they do their jobs and why it matters.

How to measure culture

Culture can be hard to measure. But it leaves clues. You'll know a strong, fit culture when you see it because:

- **Employees** proudly share stories about where they work and what they do.

- **Teams** enthusiastically support each other's efforts.

- **Leaders** communicate expectations, decisions, and changes in direction with clarity and transparency. They encourage new ideas and failing forward. They demonstrate vulnerability and a willingness to change their mind based on their employee's input. They praise effort and reward results.

If your organization is like most, you not only embrace the value of metrics—you track every metric you can. But it's only worth spending this much time tracking metrics if you're then actually using those metrics to drive better decisions and move the needle on your growth strategy.

Culture can be hard to measure, but it's not nearly as difficult as you might assume. Let's make it simpler. You don't need thirty metrics to measure the strength of your culture. You only need four:

1. **Attraction rate.** Have you ever considered why it takes so long to fill critical positions? One reason is your lack of internal candidates (see point four below). The other is likely the experience your candidates have throughout the recruiting and hiring process. Your candidate net promoter score (cNPS) measures the level of satisfaction job candidates have with your organization during their recruitment experience. When the right people don't feel pulled toward your mission or culture, and when their first impression of you—as evaluated through the recruitment experience—is less than inspiring, you attract fewer of the right people through the

door. As David Allen writes, according to the US Department of Labor, the wrong hire can cost your company at least 30% of that individual's salary. To get the right hire, you need to give the right people a reason to *join*.

2. **Retention rate.** You probably already track this as its opposite, which is turnover rate. If your best talent is sprinting for the exits, you're left with the wrong-fit talent, conflict, and presenteeism. But let's flip that number so that we're working on what we can increase, and we know that we need to: SHRM estimates the cost of replacing lost talent as anywhere from 90–200% of their annual salary. We also need to give people a reason to *stay*.

3. **Engagement rate.** Culture clashes and change resistance leave you and your teams disillusioned and unmotivated. This metric might hurt a bit. Instead of merely tracking your engagement survey scores, you need to track your *real* engagement rate, which is your employee engagement score multiplied by your participation rate. The downstream effect of low engagement is high employee relations volume—everything along your progressive discipline path, through to involuntary resignations. Dips in engagement are costing you big bucks too: Gallup finds that organizations with lower employee engagement have 18% lower productivity and 23% lower

profitability. We need to give people a reason to *contribute*.

4. **Internal hire rate (IHR).** This metric is also known as your internal fill rate (IFR). If you are unable to provide your talent with clear career paths, you're creating talent gaps, which drives up the cost to fill mission-critical positions. The inability to grow your own talent creates succession gaps in your pipeline. This is at no small cost, either: According to the Human Capital Management Institute (HCMI), not only are external hires 18% more expensive, they are also 21% more likely to leave within twelve months. We need to give people a reason to *grow*.

Four metrics to measure culture

Know your metrics...	...their opposites...	...and the costs
Attraction rate (cNPS)	Wrong-fit hires	30% of salary
Retention rate	Turnover	90–200% of salary
Engagement rate	Employee relations volume	18% lower productivity
		23% lower profitability
IHR rate	Succession gaps	18% more expensive
		21% more likely to leave

How do your numbers stack up? Focus is the key to clarity. Stay laser-focused on the metrics that move you toward a growth-ready culture and let go of those that aren't adding value.

Next, let's glimpse your future.

The role of HR

Over the past few years, I've been conducting a primary research study on the future of human resources, specifically the function's capacity and capability to support and accelerate a company's growth strategy. The findings, while interesting, have not been all that surprising:

- **Businesses value HR.** Business leaders recognize that HR plays a vital role in equipping organizations for future growth.

- **HR lacks critical capabilities.** The most critical capability the business needs from HR—the ability to think and act strategically—is also the biggest gap.

- **Businesses with gaps will fail.** If organizations do not act quickly to address the critical gaps, they could decline toward obsolescence.

These findings reveal a huge opportunity. Today, HR is primarily focused on people. After all, that's why so many of you have started referring to your HR department as the "people organization." While that's a noble focus, it's still only 25% of the story.

The business is predominantly focused on performance—bottom line, financial performance relative to quarterly and annual targets. That's why in just about every organization on the planet, there is a simmering tension between the chief financial officer and the chief HR officer. Awkward...

While HR and the business are intent on developing processes to generate consistency and efficiency, they are applying distinctly different lenses to those processes—people versus performance—which is widening the disconnect between HR and the business.

Here's where the opportunity comes in. Instead of continuing to focus solely on people or on performance as you map out your processes, focus on the sweet spot that lies at the intersection of people, process, and performance:

Purpose.

The 4Ps

The 4Ps model illustrates how the various areas of your culture come together. In the following sections, we'll explore how each of the four Ps influences your culture.

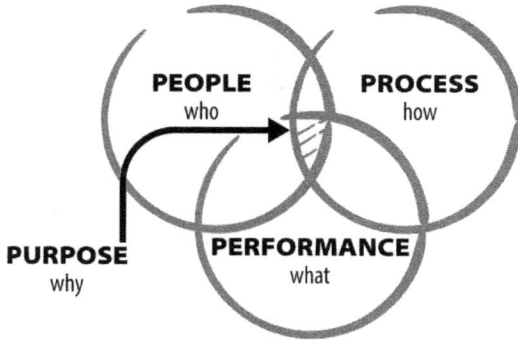

The 4Ps of culture

P1: People

Your people are your *who*. They have to be the right people, and they have to be in the right roles. It's critical to find more of the talent you need, and then put them in their fast lanes so that they feel engaged and motivated. This way, they will become so productive that your biggest challenge will be to remove obstacles and let them fly and amplify your growth. That's the path to creating *limitless talent*.

In *Change the Culture, Change the Game*, authors Roger Connors and Tom Smith challenge leaders to find ways to move people from being merely involved to being *invested*. We'll dive deeper into the concepts of limitless talent and what it means to be invested as we unpack the Growth on Purpose model in the coming chapters.

For now, understand that moving people from involved to invested requires trust. Trust is foundational to your culture, and culture is foundational to your growth. The building of trust starts before people ever join your company. If your brand promise—expressed primarily through your employer value proposition—and your onboarding experience are not aligned with your actual culture, new recruits will quickly lose trust. And once lost, trust is nearly impossible to regain.

Bottom line: To grow on purpose, you must have the right people in the right roles, with the right skills and motivation.

P2: Process

Your process is your *how*. As you grow, it's important that you have systems in place and that you incorporate structure in a meaningful and intentional way. In other words, don't introduce more bureaucracy just for the sake of saying, "We need to act more professional." Implement systems that help you replicate your best practices and enable you to hold onto what has worked well in the past, while shedding or letting go of what does not serve you. Well-designed systems and processes also help engineer out inefficiencies, which is especially important as you expand.

Getting your processes right is critical to evolving from an entrepreneurial, nimble but immature company to a professional, scalable organization. Startups and single-location companies screw this up every day. Up to the point at which they consider scaling, smaller, less mature companies memorialize everything through stories—through the personality of the founder and the core leadership team. To scale without breaking what you have already built, you must translate your best practices into systems, processes, frameworks, and standard operating procedures that help you preserve and evolve the best of what got you to this point and engineer out the rest.

Connors and Smith emphasize that the key shift within process is to move people from compliance to *commitment*. The Acceleration pillar of the Growth on Purpose model explores how to build commitment faster through gaining and nurturing trust. Trust is strengthened when there is transparency and consistency around how decisions are made, why changes happen, and how work gets done.

Bottom line: To grow on purpose, you must have systems and methods that replicate your best practices and engineer out inefficiencies.

P3: Performance

Your performance is your *what*. These are the bottom-line outcomes that your organization must accomplish. These outcomes should be ones that your people can feel good about contributing to as employees at any level of the organization, and that visibly move the needle toward your long-term growth aspirations.

Connors and Smith underscore that the key shift within performance is to move people from process to (sustained) *performance*. The Alignment pillar of the Growth on Purpose model shares ways to align your people strategy to your business strategy. For now, remember the importance of trust: Trust is embedded when there is fairness and intention in the relationship between employee and manager.

Bottom line: To grow on purpose, you must have outcomes that move the needle on your business strategy, in ways that demonstrate the behaviors you want to see repeated.

P4: Purpose

Your purpose is your *why*. This is both the sweet spot of the 4Ps of culture and the starting point of the Growth on Purpose methodology. The greatest organizations (and Simon Sinek's widespread thought leadership reinforces this), the ones that set themselves apart and position themselves for perpetual growth, are deeply connected to their why, their purpose—what they are in business to accomplish. This is the sweet spot of the 4Ps—and the starting point of the Growth on Purpose model, expressed through the Aspiration pillar—because it informs everything else. There must be a magnetic *why* that attracts the right talent, customers, and opportunities, and repels everything else.

Bottom line: To grow on purpose, you must have a magnetic mission and vision that the right talent cannot wait to contribute to fulfilling.

How to activate the 4Ps... and what *not* to do

When you merge your people, process, and performance at the sweet spot—your purpose—you will be in a far better position to grow in a sustainable way.

One caveat, though: Do not build initiatives around each of the three peripheral Ps (people, process, performance). When you do that, you continue to pull away from the center and diverge into silos. That's how we got here in the first place. Instead, focus on purpose. *Growth* on Purpose. (Did anyone else just get a James Bond vibe?)

Leaders who "get" this will drive the entire organization toward fulfillment of the growth strategy by applying the purpose filter and the Growth on Purpose methodology. They will lead the intentional and purpose-driven acquisition of the right people, design of the right processes, and recognition and reward of the right performance. As a result, their organizations will enjoy perpetual growth.

The power of questions

I'm betting you use some combination of surveys throughout your organization that are tied to specific events and HR cycles: Exit surveys when employees voluntarily resign; new hire surveys to make sure your mind-numbing orientation process hasn't irreparably disengaged your fresh talent; annual engagement surveys, because that's what everyone else is doing; and pulse surveys—which you're not sure are working, but since you can't figure out a better method of regularly "taking the temperature" of the organization, you keep doing them anyway.

Here's the thing: The feedback you get, and how actionable it is, depends on what questions you ask, in both formal surveys and informal conversations. But you don't have to wait for formal surveys to ask them.

Throughout this book, I'll share powerful questions you can ask your team and your fellow leaders to help you move the needle along your growth journey. As a starting point, I'll share some of the questions I ask prospective clients as we evaluate where they are in their strategic roadmap, and whether they are prepared to grow on purpose. Questions like:

- **How did we get here?** Where are you on your business journey? I'm interested in knowing when your business was founded, how many people you employ, your annual revenues, your average growth rate, and the average tenure of your top leadership team.

- **What's your vision?** What are the ideal outcomes you want to achieve? How big do you want this business to get, by when, and why? What will that do for your organization? What will that mean for you personally?

- **What's holding you back?** Often the biggest barriers between where you are now and where you're trying to grow are self-imposed… and not real. I like to peel back the layers and get as specific as possible on the true roadblocks to your success.

- **What are your near-term opportunities?** Assessing your ability to see—and seize— immediate opportunities will reveal how willing you are to go "all in" and commit to growing your organization on purpose.

Key takeaways

1. The world has shifted from an industrial economy to an intellectual economy, where the primary drivers of value are intangible assets: knowledge, creativity, and innovation. Leaders who can adopt a new style of leadership based on trust, collaboration, and empowerment will be the ones who succeed in the intellectual economy.

2. Culture is the foundation of a successful organization. Leaders shape culture, and culture drives success.

3. The quality of your people, the capacity and cohesion of your leaders, and the alignment of your culture with your strategy are key factors that multiply the value of your business.

4. The four key metrics for measuring the strength of your culture are attraction rate, retention rate, engagement rate, and IHR.

5. The 4Ps model of culture illustrates how the various areas of your culture come together: people, process, performance, and purpose.

Time to apply

1. What are your four key numbers?

   - Attraction rate (cNPS)

   - Retention rate

   - Engagement rate (multiplied by participation rate)

   - IHR

2. What does "owning your walk" look like for you?

3. What's one action you will take to shape your company's culture more intentionally?

TWO

How To Grow Your Business... On Purpose

Leadership Principle 3:
Leaders multiply value

In today's rapidly changing world, organizations are constantly faced with the need to grow. Whether through M&A, adding new product lines or divisions, expanding geographically, or simply becoming more professional and structured, growth is essential for survival.

Growth, though, can be a double-edged sword. For your employees, it can create opportunities to learn and develop new skills, take on new challenges, and advance their careers. For your business, it can generate increased revenue, profitability, and market share.

But when done wrong, it can lead to stress, burnout, and a loss both of a sense of belonging and of focus on what matters most.

This is where the concept of Growth on Purpose comes in. It ensures that growth is not just about getting bigger, but also about getting *better*. It is about expanding, scaling, evolving, building, maturing, and developing in ways that are aligned with your organization's vision, mission, and values, and that create a positive impact on employees, customers, and the wider community.

What it means to grow on purpose

For leaders, Growth on Purpose means creating a workplace that is both *high-performing* and *high-purpose*:

- A high-performing workplace is one where employees are engaged, productive, and committed to achieving your organization's goals.

- A high-purpose workplace is one where employees feel connected to your organization's mission and values.

Growth on Purpose means ensuring that your growth strategy is aligned with your people strategy. It means creating a workplace where the right talent wants to join, stay, contribute, and grow.

Intentionality and direction

Growth on Purpose is not about simply growing for the sake of growing. It is about growing with intentionality and direction. This means having a clear understanding of *why* your organization is growing, *what* you hope to achieve by growing, and *how* growth will impact your employees.

It also means being mindful of the potential negative impacts of growth. For example, rapid growth can lead to a loss of culture, a decline in employee morale, and an increase in turnover. Awareness—which we will explore more deeply in this book—of the risks and rewards that come with growth is the key to seeing around corners, removing obstacles, and unlocking limitless talent. The more aware you are of the potential negative impacts, the more clearly and confidently you can take the right steps to mitigate them.

Your role in Growth on Purpose

As a leader, you play a critical role in ensuring that growth is aligned with your organization's people strategy and multiplying the value of your business. The best way to do that is through activities that develop, strengthen, and nurture a talent and HR infrastructure that supports growth, including:

- Clearly articulating your organization's purpose

- Aligning HR practices with the purpose

- Creating a culture of high performance

- Investing in employee development

- Fostering a sense of community

- Providing opportunities for employees to contribute to your organization's purpose

When you're able to create a workplace that is both high-performing and high-purpose, you help ensure that growth is not just about getting bigger, but also about getting better. You can create a workplace where people can grow and thrive, both personally and professionally.

The Growth on Purpose model

The Growth on Purpose framework provides a road-map for building a culture that sustains growth. It's built on a firm foundation of best practices yet is flexible enough to meet you and your business where you are. It helps you chart and track your own growth journey.

By building and strengthening the methodology's four pillars—Aspiration, Awareness, Acceleration, and

Alignment—you can create an organization where employees are engaged, productive, and committed to your shared vision. The four pillars of the Growth on Purpose framework are how you build a culture that sustains growth. Below is a brief introduction to each of the pillars; we'll discuss them in greater detail throughout this book.

A1: Aspiration

Aspiration uses your magnetic *why* to attract, retain, and inspire more of the right people.

The problem: Low attraction. The right people (your "who") are not finding your company, not applying to be part of your organization, not feeling pulled toward your mission. You feel this pain through the high—and rising—cost to recruit new talent.

The cause: You're not giving the right talent a magnetic reason to join, so you need to strengthen your Aspiration pillar.

Aspiration: When you implement the Aspiration pillar, you create a "magnetic purpose" that makes it easy for the right talent to see why they should join your company. In the Aspiration chapter of this book, we'll dive into ways to get the right talent lined up at your door, pre-sold on working with you.

A2: Awareness

Awareness enables you to replicate your best performers and create fast lanes to turn potential into performance.

The problem: Low retention. You've managed to find (at least some of) the right people, but they don't stay long enough to give your growth strategy any momentum. High turnover costs real dollars in numerous areas—from replacement costs to lost productivity to shrinking competitiveness.

The cause: You're not giving your people a compelling reason to stay, so you need to enhance your Awareness pillar.

Awareness: Shoring up your Awareness pillar leads to "limitless talent": When your individual employees all operate within their fast lanes, they feel more empowered and motivated to stay with your company. In the Awareness chapter, we'll uncover how to get more of the right talent in the right roles to achieve your organizational purpose.

A3: Acceleration

Acceleration increases trust in leadership and strengthens team dynamics so you can solve bigger problems faster.

The problem: Low engagement. Your employees do not feel motivated to give all their love to a company that doesn't love them back. The cost of high presenteeism—where your people go through the motions and do just enough not to get fired—can be enormous.

The cause: Your people don't trust your leaders. Maybe you've asked them to participate in your annual engagement survey and failed to act on their input. Or perhaps they provided feedback to their direct manager and suffered repercussions. You might even have some leaders with a "Do as I say, not as I do" philosophy. For whatever reason, you're not filling your people with a strong desire to contribute, so you need to build trust through the Acceleration pillar.

Acceleration: Installing the Acceleration pillar creates cultural cohesion, which gives people a reason to contribute to your company. The Acceleration chapter shares ideas for strengthening and integrating your culture in ways that amplify growth.

A4: Alignment

Alignment plots the trajectory that will achieve your growth outcomes with focus, commitment, and precision.

The problem: Low IHR. You have vacancies in critical roles and not enough of the right talent to fill them. Your vast succession gaps not only create a leaky talent pipeline, they virtually assure the failure of your growth strategy and the eventual death of your business.

The cause: Your people don't feel a strong, tangible connection between where you're trying to go and why it should matter to them. They don't see a reason to grow—either themselves, or your business. You need to fortify your Alignment pillar.

Alignment: The Alignment pillar is the culmination of the three pillars that precede it. It gives your people a path toward growing themselves and your business, which is the only way to fulfill your growth strategy. In the Alignment chapter, we'll explore how to do this in predictable and repeatable ways, so you can build a talent pipeline that nourishes itself.

These four pillars will drive your organization toward perpetual growth. When you implement them, you will have an organizational culture that underpins your growth strategy, so that you can rely upon the growth you're pursuing.

This framework can feel overwhelming at first. It's important to layer it on top of your existing people strategy so you can fortify the areas that need the most support and double-down in places where you are already strong. When you drill into the four pillars, and the components within each, you can typically pinpoint the key areas that are tripping you up the most.

Growth on Purpose assessment

If you don't measure it, you can't move it. The Growth on Purpose methodology is designed to meet you where you are, build upon what's already working well, and identify specific actions to address your most critical gaps.

Before proceeding, take a few minutes to complete the Growth on Purpose assessment at www.growthonpurpose.com/assessment. It takes about five minutes to benchmark your current strengths and opportunities, so you know where you can generate quick wins and where you need to focus deeper attention.

The payoffs of Growth on Purpose

Imagine a world where your organization can achieve its full potential. A world where employees are engaged and motivated, and where leaders are able to create a culture of trust and collaboration. A world where your company is constantly growing and innovating.

This is the world that the Growth on Purpose model helps you create. By applying the four pillars of this framework, you can build a culture that sustains growth.

The Growth on Purpose model is based on the belief that growth is not just about having the right products or services; it is also about having the right people, culture, and strategy. When you solidify all four pillars, you create a culture that sustains growth over the long term. This model is a powerful tool for creating a better future for all of us. When organizations thrive, they create jobs, generate wealth, and contribute to the overall wellbeing of society. Apply this model and help create a world where every person and every organization has the opportunity to reach their full potential.

The rest of this book provides a deep dive into the four pillars. Each chapter includes recommended actions for that pillar which, together, form an integrated talent ecosystem that will help you harness your limitless talent and bulletproof your growth. We will build out that ecosystem as you progress through this book.

When you get the right talent to join your business and give them a reason to stay, they will want to contribute. The more they contribute, the more they—and your business—will grow. The more they grow, the longer they will stay. They will tell their friends about their experience, which will in turn encourage more of the right people to join. This is the virtuous cycle mentioned above:

- By giving people a reason to **join**, you entice and invite the right talent to enthusiastically want to work with you. That creates a *differentiated culture*.

- By giving your people a reason to **stay**, you have more of the right talent in place to fulfill your purpose. That builds *driven commitment*.

- By giving people a reason to **contribute**, you create a strong, fit, and integrated culture that amplifies growth. That establishes *deep connection*.

- And by giving people a reason to **grow**, you have a talent pipeline that nourishes itself. That ensures *dependable continuity*.

When you clarify your purpose, you can galvanize your culture. That's the key to multiplying the value of your business. *That's* Growth on Purpose.

Key takeaways

1. Growth on Purpose means creating a workplace that is both high-performing—where employees are engaged, productive, and committed to achieving your organization's goals—and

high-purpose, where employees feel connected to your organization's mission and values.

2. As a leader, your role in multiplying the value of your business includes clearly articulating your organization's purpose, aligning HR practices with the purpose, creating a culture of high performance, investing in employee development, fostering a sense of community, and providing opportunities for employees to contribute to achieving your organization's purpose.

3. The four pillars of the Growth on Purpose framework are Aspiration, Awareness, Acceleration, and Alignment.

4. The payoffs of Growth on Purpose are differentiated culture, driven commitment, deep connection, and dependable continuity.

Time to apply

1. Calculate your current Growth on Purpose score at www.growthonpurpose.com/assessment.

2. Think about how you can use your leadership role to multiply the value already in your business.

ASPIRATION

THREE
Aspiration

The first pillar, Aspiration, demands that you use your magnetic "why" to attract, retain, and inspire more of the right people. You need to have clear, powerful, and magnetic answers to questions like: Why does your organization exist? Why does it matter? Why should people care?

Some of the most successful companies in the world don't advertise.

Mark Shrayber lists Krispy Kreme, Trader Joe's, and Costco as companies that don't run TV commercials. Yet everyone knows someone who drives out of their way to Krispy Kreme for warm glazed donuts, to Trader Joe's for organic pancake mix, or to Costco for a 10-pound jar of mayonnaise.

It's not just their products that make these companies memorable. It's their staff. I have yet to meet a cranky employee of any of those companies. They're not just nice; they're knowledgeable, helpful, and genuine. Where do they find these people?

They don't. These people find them.

The best companies in the world attract the right people into their orbit not because they pin their mission statement on the wall and require everyone to adhere to it, but because they demonstrate their mission and their beliefs every day through their products, their services, and especially their people.

If you want to become a company that doesn't need to advertise, create an organizational culture that the right people *can't resist*.

Why would you pin your mission statement on the wall, rather than embed your purpose in every employee? What if, instead of searching high and low for the right talent to join your organization, they were actively and enthusiastically searching for *you*?

Clarity and stability

Leadership Principle 4:
Leaders light the way

In a world that is constantly changing, your employees crave stability. Not sameness; stability. Clarity in direction and consistency in decision-making. If that sounds simple to you… why are your leaders making it more difficult?

You and your fellow leaders play a critical role in providing clarity and direction. You set the tone for the organization and help everyone understand what is expected of them. One of the most important ways that leaders can light the way is by setting clear expectations. Expectations are the foundation upon which all else is built. They provide a roadmap for success and help everyone stay on track.

When you set clear expectations, you're essentially saying, "This is what we are trying to achieve. This is what 'done' looks like." You're providing a clear picture of the desired outcome and helping everyone understand their role in achieving it. When you get this right, you create a sense of alignment and purpose. Not only do you delineate what's important and how each person can contribute to your organization's success; you also create a sense of accountability, because everyone knows what you expect of them.

In addition to setting clear expectations, leaders also need to be role models. You need to demonstrate the behaviors you want to see from others. The archaic "Do as I say, not as I do" leadership style isn't going to cut it. You need to be visible and accessible, and you need to be willing to listen to and accept feedback.

In the context of the intellectual economy, it is especially important for leaders to set clear expectations for performance. In an economy where knowledge and creativity are the primary drivers of value, it is not always easy to define what "done" looks like. But it's essential that you provide guidance and support so that every employee—and consequently, your organization—can achieve their full potential. There has never been a more important time to create a culture of high performance and high purpose.

The "before" state: Low attraction

When the Aspiration pillar is missing, people don't understand the journey you're on. They're not pulled into your orbit. And because they don't relate to your mission or your why, they don't believe in you. They don't see where they belong, and they don't believe in the value proposition you're selling. So they never join.

Solve the headache... and open the floodgates

I get migraines. Not often, but when I do get one, it's highly disruptive. It begins with blind spots in my vision, and once those set in, I have to pop an aspirin as quickly as possible, then sit in a dimly lit room until my vision clears.

When your people lack clarity around your organizational purpose, their vision of where you're trying to grow gets cloudy too. And until it clears, it impedes their ability to dig in, lean in, and give you their best effort and ideas.

In *Atlas of the Heart*, Brené Brown addresses the difference between fitting in (conformity) and belonging (community). Your employees want to work in an organization where they can truly be themselves (authenticity), not fit themselves into a tightly lidded box. So stop asking for entrepreneurial spirit and then penalizing those employees for owning their walk. Instead, attract the right talent to your door and show them the journey that awaits them. The easiest way to do that is by installing the Aspiration pillar within your business.

The Aspiration pillar

As an organization, you must have a magnetic *why*. A purpose. A mission and a vision. Something that, at your core, is so attractive to the right talent that they can't help but lean in and want to take part in it. It's vital that you get crystal clear about why you're in business in the first place, why your leadership role exists, and what you're striving to accomplish over the long term. Aspirational clarity is what pulls the right people into your orbit and makes them want to be part of your journey.

To increase your employees' sense of belonging—that they are in the right organization and can be fully themselves—you must give them reasons to believe. The best way to do that is through your mission, vision, and values.

I read a quote many years ago that stayed with me: "Your mission pushes you, your vision pulls you, and your values keep you from veering off the road." I can't remember (nor can I locate) the author of that quote. And perhaps that's the key point here: The messages that resonate must have a longer shelf life than their creators.

This applies in business. Your mission, vision, and values must outlast your tenure as a leader if they are to galvanize your culture and enable perpetual growth.

Think of Martin Luther King, Jr., for example. As soon as you hear his name, you immediately think, "I have a dream." His message was so powerful, so resonant, so visionary, that it has only gained in volume in the decades since he delivered it.

What will your message be? Does your organizational purpose have the power and the potential to outlast you?

Your purpose is your North Star. It is the unique and carefully nurtured combination of your mission, your vision, and your values. It's your "stake in the ground" about who you are, why you're in business, what you stand for and against, and where you're striving to grow. Your mission, vision, and values are what drive you, hold you accountable, attract the right talent and opportunities and turn away the wrong ones. Let's explore each of them in turn.

A mission that pushes you

What's your company's mission? Before you look up your mission statement on your company website or on the framed poster on your office wall, listen up: Your mission statement is not the same as your mission. Your mission statement is what you paid an agency to dream up so that you had something flowery to show your shareholders, your community, and the casual visitors to your website and headquarters.

Your *mission* is your organization's reason for being. It is the *why* behind everything you do today. It provides a sense of purpose and direction, and it helps to motivate and inspire employees. Until you embed your true mission into every employee, your "mission statement" is not worth the paper (digital or otherwise) it's printed on.

Your mission is the powerful force that propels your organization forward. For example, the mission of TED is "to spread ideas." The mission of Zappos is "to deliver WOW through service." And the mission of Oscar Mayer is "to get a better hot dog in every hand."

Your mission must make your employees hungry. Not necessarily for hot dogs, but for enthusiastically contributing their best ideas, talents, and energies toward fulfilling your purpose.

Like your vision, your mission must outlive your tenure. Think of President John F Kennedy's challenge to America in 1961 that we would put a person on the Moon before the end of the decade. We did, in 1969... almost six years after he died. His mission was so compelling, so ambitious, and so magnetic that people continued to work together to fulfill it, even after Kennedy was gone.

If a mission falls in the woods, does it make a sound?

Several years ago, I began working with a regional president of a large environmental company. He had spent his entire career in the industry, and over the previous couple of decades he had ascended in his current organization. He was preparing to take on his next assignment, which was to oversee the turnaround of the company's highest-profile division. He would be accountable for managing a $70m operating budget and motivating a 200-person workforce. He needed to identify his best strategy for achieving his mission, and quickly assess his new team's ability and willingness to contribute to it.

But first, he needed to overcome his assumption that everyone was clear on the mission.

When we first started working together, I asked him a simple question:

"Does everyone on your team understand the mission of the company?"

He replied, "Well, they'd better... Even before I moved into this position, I have been part of the executive leadership team that went out and communicated the mission over the past few months."

I asked him, "What did that process look like?"

"We did road shows," he responded. "We met with small groups of employees at every work location, and we shared the mission, vision, and values."

"OK," I said. "Let me reflect that back to you. You went *out*, and you communicated *out* the mission, vision, and values. Is that right?"

"Yup."

"So..." I continued. "How did you confirm that the employees 'got it'"? How did you have them report back to you and the other executive leaders what they believed your mission, vision, and values to be?"

Silence.

Many leaders skip the step of verifying that their people understand the mission. They try to move directly into action planning and execution, and then they are astounded when they meet cultural resistance at every turn.

Getting mission clarity is the fundamental first step to assembling the right team, placing them into the right roles, and mobilizing them to work together to execute the strategy for growing your business.

As I worked with this leader, he took a step back from his strategic plan and spent the first thirty days in his new role meeting with his employees. He reiterated the mission of the company, and their division's role in contributing to it. And then he listened. He adjusted his message. And he listened some more. Over time, his employees were able to understand and *believe* in their shared mission.

Within the first six months in his leadership role, he and his team achieved an 18% increase in business profitability.

Our ongoing work includes regular sounding board sessions to review his strategy, conduct preventive maintenance, and make any necessary course corrections. Our goal is to maintain his balanced perspective, mission clarity, and confident decision-making, by continually finding ways to replicate his team's wins and mitigate their challenges.

A vision that pulls you

Renowned thought leader Simon Sinek deeply believes—and I wholeheartedly agree—that your "why" sets you apart. As Sinek explains in *Start with Why*, every organization knows *what* it does, and *how* it does it. But the truly differentiated organizations understand *why* they exist.

A differentiated *why* doesn't just set you apart from your competitors. It serves as the beacon that attracts the right talent into your orbit. Your vision is the organization's desired future state. It's not where you are today, but what you aspire to become. It pulls you through the daily firefighting, the quarterly financial reckoning, and the annual performance evaluations by reminding you of the mark you're striving to leave on the world. A clear vision helps to focus efforts and ensure that everyone is working toward the same goals.

The vision of an organization provides a sense of hope and optimism. For example, Kellogg's vision is "a good and just world where people are not just fed but fulfilled." The vision of the World Health Organization is "a world in which everyone can live healthy, productive lives." And Netflix's vision is "to entertain the world."

Your vision must be clear and ambitious. It must provide direction, motivation, and inspiration for the right talent to join your cause. When people work toward a shared vision, they are more likely to be motivated and engaged in their work—and that leads to increased productivity and innovation.

Values that keep you from veering off the road

The values of your organization are the guardrails that keep your people and your business from wandering into a ditch. They're the guiding principles that govern how you behave and how you get things done. They provide a trustworthy framework for decision-making and help ensure that your organization remains true to your mission. Strong values help to build trust and credibility, and provide stability during times of change.

For example, Patagonia's core values are "quality, integrity, environmentalism, justice," and—my personal favorite—"not bound by convention." Indeed. Patagonia has been around for over fifty years, and they recently refreshed their values to those listed here. Even a well-established and highly respected brand understands the need to re-evaluate and evolve their values to make sure they continue to align with the culture they're trying to shape.

I'm tempted to slap a big, red warning label on this section, because your values are your biggest clue to current and prospective employees about what your culture *really* is. If there is the slightest disconnect between what you *say* your organizational culture is all about and what your leaders *do*—in terms of how you behave, what you reward, and what you tolerate—people will believe what you *do* over what you *say*. Never forget that.

What Aspiration looks like

There are so many ways you can deliver aspirational clarity to the right talent. Here are four actions to get you started.

1. MVV refresh

Your mission, vision, and values (MVV) are the foundational elements of your Aspiration pillar. Take a fresh look at them. Do they still represent your culture, your beliefs, and your growth philosophy? If they don't, then it's time to refresh them. Don't do this in a vacuum. Pull together a cross-section of employees at all levels of your organization and re-evaluate your purpose. Crowdsourcing your refreshed MVV is powerful because people support what they help to create. Pulling together a carefully curated group of talent is also a great way to strengthen cultural cohesion, as we'll explore in the Acceleration chapter. Just make sure to facilitate the conversation in an intentional way: While including others in this process increases engagement, it can also devolve into chaos if you're not careful. Start with the end in mind, determine the "end state" you ultimately want to land on, and facilitate the discussion toward that goal.

Once your MVV accurately reflect your culture and strategy, it's time to double-down on them. Integrate them into your talent strategy, including your performance management process, recognition program, and development opportunities. Promote them on your website. Include them in your job postings and other candidate outreach.

Never let your MVV grow stale again. Review them at least every three years. Compare what they stand for with what you are tolerating. Verify that you are holding all leaders and employees accountable for demonstrating, defending, and nurturing them. Check in with your employees to confirm that everyone still believes in, understands, and embraces your MVV. If not, it's time for another refresh.

2. Talent Principles

While you're gathering talent to refresh your MVV, it's a great time to pressure-test your Talent Principles. These are a high level set of statements that establish a common language of talent for your organization. They express who you are as a business, what you stand for, and what you stand against. They clearly articulate the commitments your organization is making to the right talent, and what that talent can expect from a career at your company if they dedicate their time and talents. They also hold all people leaders accountable to the same guidelines and guardrails for identifying, motivating, and nurturing talent within their teams.

3. Talent Value Proposition

I won't go into detail here about what an employee value proposition is. If you've been a leader for even ten minutes, you know that it's essentially the promise you make to prospective employees about all the great benefits, experiences, and rewards they can expect if they decide to join your company. But I do want to challenge you to think of it as your Talent Value Proposition (TVP). Because you want to be in the business of attracting, retaining, and harnessing the right talent toward fulfillment of your purpose.

I also want to challenge you to do everything within your power to ensure there is zero discrepancy between the promises you make through your TVP and the promises you keep through your actual culture. A strong TVP is essential for business success. But just like a chain, it's only as strong as the weakest element of your culture. If you make a bold promise to attract top talent through your TVP, only to renege on that promise once they join your team and experience your culture, you will not only lose that talent, you will damage your brand reputation and your ability to attract talent in the future.

Before you reassure me that your TVP is perfectly aligned with your culture, ask yourself a few questions:

- Do your job postings advertise for people with "entrepreneurial spirit"?

  - Do you hold your new hires strictly accountable to the bullets on their job description, or do you invite them to apply their out-of-the-box expertise to go beyond those essential functions?

- Do you describe your work environment as a place where people can bring their full, authentic selves to work?

  - Do you adapt the job role to fit the best talents and strengths of the unique individual, or do you expect them to adapt their uniqueness to fit the role?

- Do you pride yourself on empowering your employees to be innovative and take risks?

  - Do you reward them for failing forward, or do you deduct from their bonus when their innovative idea falls short?

If your answers reveal some discrepancies, don't beat yourself up. You're not the only organization making promises that your organization isn't keeping. But you *are* the leader reading this book. And now that you can see it, you can't ignore it, so let's do something about the disconnect.

I'm not suggesting you water down your TVP. Keep making bold promises. Just make sure you and your fellow leaders shape your culture so that you live up to them.

4. Message mapping

Once you have refreshed your MVV, identified a set of Talent Principles that establish a common language of talent and hold all people leaders accountable, and created a TVP that delivers on your brand promise, it's time to map out a set of consistent, aligned messages to all categories of stakeholders—both internal and external to your organization—so you attract the right talent and keep your existing talent on the right path. A message map is a powerful tool that translates all the above actions into simple, straightforward talking points. It ensures that you and your fellow leaders are communicating with clarity, consistency, and authenticity—and that you are honoring the commitments you make to your current and future employees.

If you'd like a simple format for bringing this message map to life, you can download a free template at www.growthonpurpose.com/resources.

The "ideal" state: Magnetic purpose

Through completing the four actions above, you take aspiration from a theoretical concept to a magnetic purpose: A compelling message and brand based on your "why." Once you have a refreshed MVV; a set of Talent Principles; and a compelling (and accurate) Talent Value Proposition, you will quickly differentiate yourself from your competition and entice the right talent to line up outside your door, pre-sold on working with you. And the more aligned your communications are with your purpose, the faster and more reliably you will increase employee retention, employee engagement, and employer brand reputation.

When you get the Aspiration pillar right, you give people a reason to join you and can build a truly differentiated culture.

MVV Refresh

Talent Principles

Talent Value Proposition

Message Mapping

ASPIRATION

Powerful questions

Below are some questions to ask yourself, your colleagues, and your employees that will create aspirational clarity:

- Why did you join this company?

- Why do you stay?

- What are you proud of achieving in your role and with your team?

- What do you wish more employees and job candidates knew about your company?

- What do you like best about working at your company?

- Why does your company exist? What is it in business to accomplish?

- How does your company make a difference in the world?

Key takeaways

1. Leaders light the way by setting clear expectations and being role models.

2. The Aspiration pillar serves as the North Star for your organization, pulling the right talent into your orbit.

3. Mission, vision, and values are critical components of Aspiration, defining your purpose, desired future, and guiding principles.

   - A mission is not just a statement. It's the organization's reason for being, driving purpose and motivating employees.

   - A vision is the desired future state, providing direction, focus, and inspiration.

- Values act as guardrails, guiding behavior and decision-making to ensure alignment with the mission.

4. Aspirational clarity creates a sense of belonging and helps employees understand their role in the organization's success.

Time to apply

1. Review your Aspiration score within your Growth on Purpose assessment scorecard. Commit to taking one action to improve your score within this pillar.

2. Ask your employees each of the "powerful questions" listed above. Do not conduct a survey; just incorporate them, one or two at a time, into the conversations you're already having with your people. For example:

   - At the beginning of each team meeting, ask one of these powerful questions.

   - Use the responses to your questions to refine your magnetic purpose. Make sure your purpose includes clear, compelling, powerful answers to: Why does your organization exist? Why does it matter? Why should people care?

3. What's one way you can strengthen your ability to keep the promises your Talent Value Proposition is making?

4. What's driving you and your business today? What's drawing your gaze toward the horizon? What beliefs do you hold as sacred?

5. What's one action you will take to "light the way" for your team?

FOUR

Awareness Of Self

I n building the second pillar, Awareness, you're trying to replicate your best performers and create fast lanes to turn potential into performance. This requires you to define and measure what unique talents every person in your organization can contribute toward achieving your purpose.

The 2011 film *Limitless*, starring Bradley Cooper, was based on the premise that humans use a shockingly small percentage of our brain capacity. By taking a magic pill, Cooper's character was able to access 100% of his brain, which enabled him to achieve genius levels of performance, and all the riches and romance that came with it. It was an underrated addition to the Alice in Wonderland-style, "blue pill vs red pill" movie genre that includes *The Matrix*, *Lucy*, *Inception*, and others.

I could talk about movies (and '80s music trivia) all day. But I'll resist that rabbit hole and get to the point: Everyone is looking for the magic pill that will transform average humans into superheroes. Including you, dear leader. The reality is that the talent within your organization is limited. It's finite. It's exhaustible. (And it's likely exhausted.)

It's not unlimited. But it can be limitless.

What would your organization look like if it was stocked with limitless talent? This chapter will show you how to remove the obstacles that are holding your talent back.

Feeding your passion

Leadership Principle 5:
Leaders feed their passion

Let's talk about your "why" for a moment.

Not your organization's why. We covered that in detail in the previous section. *Your* why. The reason your role as a leader exists. The reason *you* show up in that leadership role every day. What's your why?

As a leader, it's your job to put your people in the best position to succeed. In reality, you're constraining your employees, their pathways, and their "walk" more often than you think. One of the most common ways leaders do this is by limiting people to the bullets in their job description. Another is by extinguishing their enthusiasm… and suppressing your own.

Your energy—both positive and negative—infects others, so be mindful of your energy and be intentional about feeding it. Feeding your passion includes nurturing your talent. Start by increasing awareness of who you have and what they possess. Then you can put more of the right people into their fast lanes so that they are more productive and engaged, which in turn makes your business more profitable.

The "before" state: Low retention

Your people can't see a clear path for their own career growth because it's clogged with roadblocks, so they don't see a reason to stay.

If you're doing exit surveys—and actually studying the trends they reveal—you're likely finding that the top reason people voluntarily leave your company is a lack of development opportunities. They don't see a clear career path. In other words, since they don't see how they can grow, they can't find a reason to stay.

So give them one.

The real cost of the lost

Many credible resources, such as SHRM, remind us that it costs 90–200% of a person's annual salary to replace them. But what does that mean in real life?

The National Football League has a "hard cap" on each team's salary budget for a season. The team can spend up to the salary cap on players, but not over. If a team wants to replace a player who is injured or retiring, they need to find a new player who is willing to play for the same amount of money or less. This can be difficult, because the new player knows that the team has a limited budget and is desperate to find someone to replace the lost player.

Now imagine that a team's quarterback is injured and needs to be replaced. The quarterback is the most important player on the team, so the team is willing to pay a premium to replace him. The team finds a new quarterback who is willing to play for $20 million per season, even though the injured quarterback was only making $10 million per season. This means that the team must spend twice as much money to replace the injured quarterback.

Since I'm betting you hold onto your annual salary budget more tightly than Jerry Jones holds onto his head coach's contract, you're in the same boat. When you lose a key employee, you have to spend time and money recruiting, hiring, and training their replacement—who might also demand a higher salary than the previous employee, because they know your company needs them.

In addition to the financial cost, there is also a non-financial cost to replacing people. The new employee may not be as productive as the previous one, and it may take time for them to learn the ropes and develop chemistry with their teammates. This can lead to a decrease in performance for the team as a whole.

For a team in the NFL, this might mean that they lose games and fail to make the playoffs. This could have a significant financial impact on the team, as they would miss out on revenue from ticket sales, merchandise sales, and television contracts.

What game will your company lose if you choose the wrong talent, or fail to retain the *right* talent?

The game of talent

I love spending time with my nephews, especially when they ask me to play an "old school" game like Mastermind. It's a nice break from Xbox, which I can't quite grasp (I grew up playing Pong and Atari).

If you're unfamiliar, Mastermind is a two-player game that involves one player lining up four pegs of varying colors at their end of the board, hidden from the other player. The other player then gets several attempts to guess the correct order and color of the opponent's pegs. The opponent then scores each guess by indicating how many pegs are the wrong color and in the wrong hole, the right color in the wrong hole, and the right color in the right hole. You win the game if you can put all four of the right colors in the right holes before you run out of guesses.

The game of talent is eerily similar to Mastermind:

- Sometimes you have the wrong people in the wrong roles (wrong color peg, wrong hole).

- Sometimes you have the right people in the wrong roles (right color peg, wrong hole).

- You win the game when you have the right people in the right roles (right color peg, right hole).

If you're struggling to find more people, you're missing the point of the game. You don't need to look for *more* people; you need to look for the *right* people. You need to place them in the right roles, and you need to give them a reason to stay. The best way to do that is through the Awareness pillar.

The Awareness pillar

Awareness of self—as individual employees, as leaders, and as an organization—shines a light on what you have and what you lack. Once you have self-awareness, you will be much surer footed along your path to sustainable growth.

It's not enough to *attract* talent. This is where a lot of organizations go down the wrong path. They think, "If we just go out and hire the best talent, they're going to figure out how to make us successful."

You don't want to look for the best talent; you want to look for the *right* talent.[1] And you can't then assume that the right talent is simply going to figure out their own way: The "plug and play" candidate does not exist. You have to put your people in the best position to operate in their fast lanes and play to their strengths. That not only requires awareness of what those strengths and fast lanes are, it often requires you to be flexible in the roles you define for them, because it is far easier to change the role than it is to change the person.

---

1   A brief rant about the difference between hiring the best talent and the right talent: Too often when organizations are hiring salespeople, they poach the "rockstar" from their competitor and then wonder why that rockstar underperforms in their culture. The answer is simple: Your culture is different. The cohesion on your team is different. The moving pieces are different. Aspirational clarity is a way for you to be sure you're attracting the right talent. Because not every "rockstar" can take you where you're trying to go. It's a lot easier to discern the right talent from the wrong-fit talent if you're crystal clear on your aspiration, and if you're intentional about how you build and nurture your culture.

Tapping into genius

Born Robert Schirokauer, Dr Robert S Hartman fled from Nazi Germany and dedicated his life to study-ing the structure of value and the knowledge of good. Nominated for the Nobel Peace Prize in 1973, he is considered the "father of formal axiology." He believed that everyone has a unique set of values and decision-making patterns that drive their behav-ior and motivation. His work laid the foundation for Jay Niblick's *What's Your Genius* study, which found that all "genius-level" performers—i.e., people who achieve success almost effortlessly—share two traits in common:

- Self-awareness: They have a deep understanding of what their natural strengths are (and what they're not), why they're motivated to use those talents, and how they tend to use them.

- Authenticity: They intentionally incorporate their greatest natural talents into what they do and how they do it—i.e., spending as much time as possible in their "fast lanes" or "genius zones."

The good news is that anyone can acquire these two traits. The bad news is that most organizations don't focus their attention on helping their employees to acquire them. But doing so is easier than you think: You simply need to give your employees a reason to believe.

Self-belief is the degree of confidence we have in our ability to achieve our goals. It is essential for employee empowerment, as it gives people the motivation to take on new challenges and to persevere in the face of setbacks.

Here are a few simple ways you and your fellow leaders can help your employees increase their self-belief:

- Provide them with regular feedback and recognition.
- Give them opportunities to learn and grow.
- Empower them to make decisions and take ownership of their work.
- Create a supportive and encouraging work environment.

There are also a variety of diagnostic tools that you can use to measure employee engagement and identify any flight risks. These tools can help you to understand the root causes of employee disengagement and develop targeted interventions.

An integral part of my client advisory work is a suite of battle-tested, science-backed, and EEO (Equal Employment Opportunity)-compliant diagnostic tools. I have been using these tools for over a decade and they continue to fuel many of the foundational elements of my programs. If you're interested in test driving the diagnostic tools I use, refer to the end of this book for more details.

Finding and placing the right talent

Finding the right talent requires you to look beyond resumes and job descriptions. Instead, focus on finding people who have the skills, mindset, and values to be successful in your organization.

One way to do this is to incorporate assessments that identify a candidate's fast lanes and motivations. This means focusing on the candidate's strengths and how they can be used to benefit the company, rather than looking for a perfect match to the job description. When there is strong alignment between what they are passionate about and what your organization values, retention and engagement rates are higher, and their contributions increase significantly.

Once you have found the right talent, you need to put them in the best position to succeed. This means adapting the role to fit their fast lanes. Everyone has their own fast lanes: The areas where they are naturally talented and motivated. When people are working in their fast lanes, they are more likely to be successful and productive.

To identify someone's fast lanes, you can talk to them about their interests, skills, and experience. You can also observe them at work to see what they are good

at and what they enjoy doing. Once you know someone's fast lanes, you can start to adapt their role to
fit them. This may involve changing the job description, the team they work on, or the projects they are
assigned to.

Many organizations try to change their employees to
fit the role. This is a mistake. It is much more effective
to adapt the role to fit the employee. When you try
to change an employee, you are essentially trying to
change their personality. This is difficult to do and is
likely to lead to frustration and resentment. Instead,
focus on adapting the role to fit the employee's
strengths and weaknesses.

Like viagra for engagement

I was working with the head of human resources for a
healthcare business that had recently combined two
regional competitors into one company. The two legacy
cultures could not have been more different: One was
nimble, entrepreneurial, and lacking in any structure
or best practices; the other was bureaucratic, slow to
innovate, and rigid in its structure and rules. It was
hardly a surprise, then, that the first two years post-
merger were fraught with culture clashes, high turnover,
siloed thinking, and loss of market share.

The head of HR had stepped into her leadership role at
a time when the HR organization had a 30% vacancy
rate, primarily in leadership positions—and those who
remained were deeply mistrusting of each other. In fact,

their recent engagement survey had revealed an overall engagement score of only 27%.

Over the next ninety days, we met with each member of the existing team, as well as key leaders throughout the business, to understand what they needed from each other and from the organization to advance their careers, support the team, and grow the business. We worked with the HR team to co-create a refined organizational structure that more equitably allocated resources, more clearly showed the HR team a career path, and more strongly aligned with the needs of the business. We assessed the members of the team to identify their natural strengths and motivations, so the HR leader could reassign, reallocate and, in some cases, gracefully exit resources. I then facilitated a workshop to increase the team's awareness of their own strengths and the strengths of their colleagues, improve the team's cohesion and collaboration, and enhance their ability to execute on the HR operating plan.

The annual engagement survey told the story: The team's overall engagement skyrocketed from 27% to 100% within twelve months.

What Awareness looks like

To play—and win—the game of talent, you need to increase self-awareness throughout your business. Here are four actions that will help you do that.

1. "A player" success blueprint

As I mentioned above, the key to winning the game is not to find *more* people; it's to find the *right* people. The good news is that unless you're starting from zero and have yet to hire an employee, you already have at least some of the right people working for you. Think about your best performers: Those who not only exceed performance expectations, but also buy into your vision, deliver outcomes that move the needle toward your mission, and behave in ways that reinforce your values. These are your "A players." Now you simply need to clone them.

It's simpler than you think. If you know who your A players are, measure what makes them consistently successful within your unique organization. (Assessment centers are fantastic for this; more on those in a moment.) Then use that "success profile" to find and develop others who possess similar "DNA," as well as to fill in any fundamental gaps.

When you evaluate a new job candidate, stop evaluating them against a job description; instead, evaluate them against your existing A players. You're not looking for the next employee. You're looking for the next "Bob" or "Jane." Once you personalize your talent search by getting super-specific about who your current A players are, you will be much better equipped to identify them when you see them.

2. Self-driven leadership

There's an old saying: "If you set out to develop everyone, you end up developing no one."

That is no longer true. As I mentioned earlier in this chapter, one of the main reasons your top talent is leaving is because they lack development opportunities. But until you do the work to map out your A players, you may not realize that you have other raw talent hiding in plain sight. By giving all employees an opportunity to convert their talents into strengths, you will increase retention and start to plug some of the holes in your talent pipeline.

That fits with a better saying: "A rising tide lifts all boats."

Create a few foundational development opportunities that every employee can access and complete at their own pace. Empower them to drive their own development, and then equip your people managers to have more productive conversations. Give them tools and talking points that make it easier to have career conversations with their people on potential next roles that align with their skills and motivations.

3. Assessment centers

Assessment tools are powerful diagnostic resources to measure not only the "DNA" of your existing

A players, but also the raw potential of others in your organization. I mentioned above the tools I use in my advisory work. When you incorporate assessment tools into assessment *centers,* you can evaluate potential, natural talents, and growth opportunities for as many of your rising talent as possible. Be intentional about whom you select and what you do with them afterward—following through builds engagement.

4. Succession management

Do you have a succession plan for every leader and key position holder in your organization? I suspect your response is some version of "Not yet; but we know we need to prioritize this."

If you truly saw this as a priority, you would have done it already. (Ouch.) Stop overcomplicating this. Grab my one-page succession plan template at www. growthonpurpose.com/resources. It's free to use and simple to complete.

Succession planning does not stop with the plan on a page. You have to go beyond succession *planning* to succession *management*. Start by narrowing your focus to the key positions that must have contingency plans and take action to identify and nurture a pipeline of ready-now and ready-next successors.

The "ideal" state: Limitless talent

By intentionally building up the Awareness pillar through the actions recommended above, you create "limitless talent": A workforce where every employee is in the right role, doing work they love, and reaching their full potential. This requires finding the right talent—not the "best" talent—and putting them in the best position to succeed. It also means adapting the role to fit their fast lanes, not trying to change the employee to fit the role. (Talk about trying to fit square pegs into round holes...) The more limits on your talent you remove, the greater their engagement will be, which leads to lower turnover, higher customer satisfaction, and increased productivity and profitability.

When your business and your individual employees all operate within their fast lanes, there is no end to what they can innovate and achieve. The more empowered and nurtured your people feel, the easier it is to build deep commitment. By giving people a reason to *stay*, you will have more of the right talent in place to fulfill your purpose.

ASPIRATION	AWARENESS
MVV Refresh	"A Player" Success Blueprint / Hiring Profiles
Talent Principles	Self-Driven Development
Talent Value Proposition	Assessment Centers
Message Mapping	Succession Planning

Powerful questions

Below are some questions to ask yourself, your colleagues, and your employees, that will build awareness of limitless talent:

- What are your natural talents?

- What motivates you to use your talents?

- How do you tend to use your talents?

- How do you prefer to communicate?

- What are your communication "must-haves" and "turn-offs"?

Key takeaways

1. Talent is finite, but it can be limitless.

2. Leaders need to feed their own passion and help their employees nurture their talent.

3. To stay motivated and engaged, employees need to see a clear path for their own growth and development.

4. The two traits all genius-level performers share are self-awareness and authenticity—and anyone can acquire those traits.

5. Leaders can help employees increase their self-belief by providing them with regular feedback and recognition, giving them opportunities to learn and grow, empowering them to make decisions and take ownership of their work, and creating a supportive and encouraging work environment.

6. The ideal outcome is to create "limitless talent": A workforce where every employee is in the right role, doing work they love, and reaching their full potential. This means finding the right talent and positioning them to succeed, adapting the role not the employee.

Time to apply

1. Review your Awareness score within your Growth on Purpose assessment scorecard. Commit to taking one action to improve your score within this pillar.

2. Identify your A players, quantify their success profile, and hire more people who possess their "DNA." This will help you to build a workforce of high performers who are well suited to your company's culture and mission.

3. Create a clear path for employee growth and development to help prevent them from leaving their jobs. Create a culture of development where employees have opportunities to learn new skills, take on new challenges, and advance their careers. This can be done through formal training programs, mentorship programs, and other initiatives that support employee development.

4. Empower employees to make decisions and take ownership of their work to increase engagement and productivity. Foster a sense of empowerment by giving employees clear goals and objectives, and then providing them with the resources and support they need to achieve them.

5. Establish a common vocabulary around your mission, success, and talent to ensure that everyone in the organization is focused on the

same goals and objectives. It will also create a
sense of shared purpose and camaraderie.

6. Tap into the genius of your employees by helping
them to identify and develop their natural
strengths so that they can work in their fast lanes.

7. Take one action to feed your own passion.

FIVE

Acceleration Of Trust

The third pillar, Acceleration, is about increasing trust in leadership and strengthening team dynamics so that you can solve bigger problems, faster. Getting this pillar in place will enable your teams to innovate, fail forward, and collaborate more effectively.

Since 1953, Charles Schulz's *Peanuts* comic has run the same football-themed strip every autumn. You know the one: It's where Charlie Brown optimistically believes he will kick a football high into the air, and enthusiastically runs toward it with unabated anticipation. And at the last moment, Lucy yanks the ball away and Charlie ends up flat on his back, hurt and despondent. Every. Time.

Every time, Charlie believes Lucy when she tells him that she won't pull away the ball. And every time, she does it anyway.

Your employees are not as idealistic, optimistic, or enthusiastic as Charlie Brown.

They stopped trying to kick the ball higher than your competitors long ago, because they stopped trusting your Lucys—your leaders.

Trust is hard to win and easy to lose

Why don't your employees trust their leaders? Why do so many of your employees seem to look for problems more eagerly than they hunt for solutions?

Leadership Principle 6:
Leaders do hard things

The minute your leaders violate *any* of the leadership principles stated in this book, they erode trust. When trust isn't present, your people are hesitant to share their ideas because they don't feel like you're listening. They're afraid to try new things because you've allowed a culture of blaming. Bottom line: You haven't given them a reason to contribute their best ideas, efforts, and talents. The more trust is eroded, the more your culture suffers—and the value of your business value decreases.

Leaders *must* instill, inspire, earn, and maintain trust. One of the fundamental ways you can do that as a leader is by demonstrating consistency between what you expect of your people… and what you demonstrate yourself. Sometimes, that feels hard to do.

Author Glennon Doyle sparked a movement with one sentence in her book *Untamed*: "We can do hard things."

Some days as a leader, there are walks you don't want to take. For me, that day was June 2, 2011. That was the day of my surgery to remove the three malignant tumors growing inside me. While I knew that having the surgery was something I had to do, when I woke up that morning, I didn't want to face it. As I was trying to remember how to breathe, and to step forward into my day, my phone rang. It was one of my close work colleagues, Treva. She wanted to wish me well and let me know she was praying for me.

Treva was calling me from her hospital bed. She had just had surgery herself two days before, for an even more sinister cancer, and was still recovering. Yet she called to reassure me that "You've got this, and I've got you." It was exactly the shot of courage I needed. If she could face her cancer, I could toughen up and face mine. So I hung up the phone, and I walked toward my day of doing hard things.

Your people need to hear this type of message too. They need to know that you and your organization have their back. And you, as a leader, need to have the right people in your corner to lift up you, your team, and your strategy.

The "before" state: Low engagement

Did you hear the one about the difference between bacon and eggs?

- To make eggs, the chicken must be involved.
- To make bacon, the pig must be committed.

If your employees aren't engaged—or, at best, they feel ambivalent about being part of your organization—then they don't "feel the love," and so they won't see a reason to contribute to your mission. As we all know, actively disengaged employees can rapidly infect your culture.

How do you move the right talent from merely being involved... to being enthusiastically committed?

Salaries lose their impact

In Ancient Rome, soldiers were paid, in part, in salt. Salt was such a rare and expensive commodity that it formed part of the soldiers' compensation—in fact, that's where the word "salary" originates.

And just as our taste buds become accustomed to salt over time, we get used to our salary; we take for granted that the chef—in this case, the employer—will apply this "ingredient" judiciously. As a leader, you must find "stickier" ways to retain, entice, mobilize, and motivate employees, over and above providing them with fair compensation. If you don't, you'll lose more than flavor. You'll lose your best employees and the momentum they generate.

Let 'em kick the ball, Lucy

Let's return to the NFL. Imagine a football team where the players are not engaged. They show up to practice late, they don't put in full effort, and they don't communicate well with each other. This team is likely to have a lot of turnovers, make a lot of mistakes, and lose a lot of games. This could lead to a decrease in the team's productivity (wins) and profitability (revenue).

Now imagine a football team where the players are highly engaged. They show up to practice early, they work hard, and they communicate effectively with each other. This team is more likely to avoid turnovers, make fewer mistakes, and win more games. And this puts them on a much surer path to the Super Bowl.

The same is true for businesses. When employees are not engaged, they are less productive and more likely to make mistakes. This can lead to a decrease in productivity (your wins) and profitability (your revenue). And that's just for starters. According to Gallup, teams with low employee engagement experience the following business outcomes:

- 18% lower productivity
- 23% lower profitability
- 81% higher absenteeism
- 18% higher turnover
- 28% higher incidence of theft
- 64% more safety incidents (accidents)
- 41% more quality defects
- 10% lower customer loyalty/engagement

If reading these statistics feels overwhelming, just imagine how overwhelmed your people managers and recruiters feel by having to fill so many vacancies over and over. Where would you prefer that your people managers spend their time: interviewing job candidates or increasing your company's profitability?

Before you invest more money in increasing your external candidate funnel, focus on improving the engagement of the people who have already agreed to work for you.

Stop incentivizing vertically

One of the most common complaints I hear from leaders is that their people don't collaborate. And I always put the same question to them: How are you incentivizing them? Are their performance objectives and bonus targets based on achieving outcomes within their *vertical* team, division, or function?

People focus on what gets reinforced and rewarded. So if you're incentivizing your people based on their vertical achievements, don't be surprised if they don't prioritize collaboration across the organization. Instead, find ways to motivate, recognize, and reward them for thinking and acting *horizontally*.

Here's another challenge: Remember how you include in every job posting that you're looking for candidates with "entrepreneurial spirit"? Be honest: What do you do when your people try out a new idea and it fails? Or when they make a mistake? Or when they demonstrate a high level of effort yet fall short of your expectations?

Organizations that grow on purpose embrace the concept of "failing forward." They recognize that you learn more from your mistakes and failures than you do when everything goes right.

Here's a radical idea: Identify one super-stretch goal for each member of your team. A goal that you co-create with your employee, ideally one that they feel passionate about working on and will have a hugely positive impact on the organization if it succeeds. If the employee succeeds, give them a significant reward. If the employee falls short on achieving the super-stretch outcome, reward their idea and effort.

Remember, this is a goal that is highly ambitious, inspires the employee to strive for innovation, and will make a big impact. That's one way to inspire and encourage failing forward.

The Acceleration pillar

While culture is foundational to your success, trust is one of the foundational elements of culture. When you see your levels of employee disengagement or turnover increase and you start losing more of the right talent, you can often trace it back to a lack of trust—between the workforce and the leadership, or across teams. To avoid this, it's important to find ways to accelerate trust.

Don't confuse "accelerating" trust with manufacturing it—i.e., faking it or trying to be something you're not. That's why it's so important to work on Aspiration and Awareness first. When you become highly attuned to what your culture is all about, and what strengths and gaps you have, you can accelerate trust by being authentic as leaders[2] and having an environment where people collaborate and support each other across teams. Without trust, you can't achieve your growth strategy.

To accelerate trust among teams, it's important to understand one another's fast lanes, motivations, and communication must-haves. This can help to reduce conflict, improve collaboration, and boost productivity.

- **Fast lanes** are the areas where people are naturally talented and motivated. When people are working in their fast lanes, they are more likely to be engaged, productive, and successful.

- **Motivations** are the reasons why people are driven to do what they do. Understanding a person's motivations can help you to communicate with them in a way that is more effective and persuasive.

- **Communication must-haves** are what people need in order to communicate effectively. These can include preferred communication channels, modes of communication, and feedback styles.

---

2   Leaders *must* lead by example. Too many leaders convince themselves that leadership is a role they play, instead of an obligation to show up with authenticity and vulnerability—i.e., with what makes them human. You don't need to be charismatic or have a "larger than life" persona to inspire people to follow you. The most followable leaders are followable because they're real—because people recognize that they're human. They're relatable and they're beautifully flawed, just like the people they lead.

Connecting whys

The "why" is such a vital driving force that we led with it in the Aspiration chapter (your organizational why), and then we got personal about it in the Awareness section (your individual why). In this Acceleration chapter, we explore how to tap into the why to speed up trust.

When people feel connected to their work and to their colleagues, they are more likely to be engaged and productive. They are also more likely to stay with the company and contribute to its long-term success.

Yet many leaders struggle to connect people to the mission, perhaps because they feel overwhelmed by the day-to-day demands of their job, or they may not know how to communicate the mission in a way that is meaningful to their employees. Here are three simple steps leaders can take to connect individuals' roles to the shared mission:

1. **Recall why you joined/stay with your company.** What is it about the mission that inspires you? Once you have a clear understanding of your own motivations, you can share them with your team members in a way that is authentic and relatable.

2. **Name your greatest role challenge.** What is the one factor or obstacle that is holding you back from being as effective in your role as you would

like to be? By sharing your own challenges, you demonstrate vulnerability with and trust in your team. This leads to a more open and honest dialogue about the challenges that everyone is facing.

3. **Understand why each role matters.** Help your employees understand the impact their work has on your company's shared mission. How does their work contribute to the success of the team and their colleagues? By helping team members to see the bigger picture, you can give them a sense of purpose and meaning in their work.

What Acceleration looks like

Accelerating trust between your leaders and your workforce, as well as across teams, is easier than you think. Here are some actions to get you started.

1. Create onboarding programs... not retention killers

According to Jane Thier in *Fortune* business magazine, most new hires start looking for their next job within the first three months of their current job. Instead of feeding that statistic, conquer it. Create onboarding programs that go beyond "check the box" paperwork and actually build enthusiasm for your company. This is a great way to start delivering on the promise you made through your Talent Value Proposition. Give your new hires a glimpse into the journey that awaits them and the culture they have an opportunity to enrich, so they never feel buyer's remorse at having accepted your employment offer.

If you would like a sample onboarding plan for inspiration, you can download my free template at www.growthonpurpose.com/resources.

2. Cross-pollinate your talent

No one intends to form silos in their business. These form over time. One of the ways to break down silos is to form coaching cohorts with employees from across your organization. Select a cross-section of people managers or individual contributors and use a coaching model to enhance their self-awareness and build their confidence and competence in public speaking, problem solving, networking, and collaboration.

You can run each cohort for three to six months—enough time to boost their skills and strengthen their network. After the coaching program ends, give them tools—such as chat apps or an internal messaging forum—that enable them to continue to network with each other, share best practices, and solve problems.

3. Strengthen team dynamics before planning your strategy

Clients often ask me to facilitate their strategic planning sessions. I will take on the challenge with one condition: First we need to spend time on team dynamics. In their haste to gain traction on their five-year strategy, leaders often skip over this step. Then they wonder why they never hit their milestones.

If your team doesn't trust one another—or you as their leader—it doesn't matter how brilliant your growth strategy is, you will fall short of achieving it.

Before jumping into building your strategy, roadmaps, and milestones, convene your team for a half- or full-day "retreat" to strengthen the team dynamics and increase their ability and willingness to collaborate and support one another.

If you'd like to see the day one agenda I use in my facilitation—which focuses on boosting collaboration and cohesion—you can download it for free at www.growthonpurpose.com/resources.

4. Get your high potentials on your radar

If you completed the actions in the Awareness section, you should have a solid list of your A players by now. And if you used assessment tools, you should also have a solid initial list of other raw talent.

Don't let those lists get stale. Turn them into your talent radar. Put as many of your A players into your A positions—the positions that have the most direct impact on your company's revenue. Create individual development plans for your A players and your high potentials and invest heavily in their development through one-on-one coaching, training opportunities, and experiential learning.

It's not enough to identify your talent. You must be strategic, intentional, and disciplined about nurturing it.

5. Raise your floor

While you're offering differentiated development to your A players and high potentials, you need to bring up the minimum proficiency level of *all* people managers.

Like most leaders, when I was first promoted into a people management position, I wasn't given a "How to be an effective manager" manual. I was thrown into the deep end and learned as I went, through many trials and a whole bunch of errors.

We can do better.

Not every people manager is suited to the role. But until you train all your people managers on the essential skills and competencies, your overall performance will suffer and you will miss some of the raw talent that could be higher performers with the right levels of competence and confidence.

Here are three simple steps to raising the minimum proficiency of all managers:

1. Make a list of your lowest-performing managers—including those with the highest rates of employee relations issues and turnover within their teams.

2. Identify their biggest skill deficits (aim for three to five).

3. Develop and deliver training modules that address those gaps.

6. Mentor in all directions

The reason many employees never receive enough learning and development is because most organizations put the full burden of delivering those opportunities onto their human resources team. Like every other department in your company, HR has finite capacity. While "build a mentoring program" may be on their list of "must do" priorities, it continues to get deprioritized in the face of other, more pressing initiatives—such as resolving employee relations issues.

Identifying, nurturing, mobilizing, and motivating talent is not a human resources function; it's the job of *every* people manager. But the capacity of people managers is also finite, so you need to get creative and stop overcomplicating this.

Many an industry superstar, from Tony Robbins to Steve Jobs, credits mentoring as one of the top secrets to their success. Stop waiting for HR to build a formal mentoring program. Your people have been asking for mentoring for years, so give it to them.

Mentoring doesn't only take the form of a formal, enterprise-wide program. Informal mentoring relationships and reverse mentoring can be even more impactful—and easier to create. There are unofficial mentors throughout your company. Get out of their way and encourage your people to find one. Help them to become more aware of their fast lanes and "non-talents" (perhaps re-read the Awareness chapter), find someone in the organization who is capable and confident in an area they want to strengthen, and agree on regular check-ins. The mentoring relationship can evolve from there. The longer you spend overcomplicating the structure, the longer it will take you to begin.

Just begin.

7. Listen for the "click"

If you spend enough time interacting with your team, eventually you will reach what I call "the moment." It happens when the people on your team break away from their preconceived idea of what motivates some-one else in the room, or from a previously held belief, and realize that a new belief frees them up to be more authentic, feel more fulfilled, and do better work within a team of people who are more like them than they had previously assumed or believed.

This is the moment when trust of others begins. It starts with what Brené Brown, in her book *Atlas of the Heart*, calls "self-trust."

Building trust to accelerate commitment

A $10 billion company brought in a new chief operating officer to achieve a set of highly ambitious objectives, including exponential growth over a five-year period. The company had recently completed a significant merger, and the COO's leadership team was a combination of both leaders from the legacy companies and a few external hires. They had never worked together before, and were tasked with delivering aggressive business results through the efforts and outputs of their workforce.

There was just one problem: Since the leadership team didn't know one another, they didn't trust one another... or the COO.

The COO hired me to facilitate a strategic road mapping workshop to help them set the interim milestones and outcomes that would progress them toward their five-year goals.

"I'm happy to facilitate that session," I said. "As day two. But we need to start by working on your team's dynamics on day one."

The COO agreed, and we got to work.

As the leaders walked into the room for day one and selected their seats, no one spoke to each other. They were tentative and suspicious about the "agenda" behind the session.

Through a combination of pre-work and interactive discussions, I helped everyone on the leadership team—including the COO—increase their self-awareness of their natural strengths, motivations, and preferred styles of operating and communicating. I created a safe, open environment in which everyone started to feel comfortable sharing candid and vulnerable insights on their own talents, blind spots, and styles. In turn, they grew more open to learning what their colleagues' "fast lanes" were, what motivated them, how they preferred to communicate, and what communication styles caused them to shut down.

By the end of day one, the team had transformed. They were more open, trusting, and supportive of each other. That evening, they lingered over their team dinner, laughing together and sharing personal stories, and they excitedly looked forward to working together.

On day two, the team got to work on their strategic roadmap. Because they had invested time on day one in deepening their connection with each other, they were able to map out what each team leader needed to accomplish over the next five years, and engage in productive, real-time negotiation and compromise on their goals. They collaborated to understand and resolve the interdependencies of their individual deliverables, instead of defending their silos and individual agendas.

By the end of day two, they had co-created a five-year strategic roadmap that they were aligned on and committed to achieving.

One of the participants remarked, "For the first time since joining this company, I don't feel alone."

The "ideal" state: Cultural cohesion

Acceleration of trust creates incredible momentum for your growth strategy—if you have the Aspiration and Awareness pillars in place. Installing the Acceleration pillar adds cultural cohesion, which delivers on the promise of your Talent Value Proposition. When you have the right combination of talent and you nurture that talent through carefully crafted onboarding programs, cohort coaching, team dynamics workshops, talent radars and differentiated development, and mentoring in all directions, you form cultural cohesion. Such cohesion is only possible when employees trust each other and their leaders, are incentivized to collaborate instead of compete, and feel empowered to work together to solve the organization's biggest hurdles to long-term productivity, profitability, and growth.

When you get the Acceleration pillar right, you create deep connection. By giving people a reason to contribute, you will have a strong, fit, and integrated culture that amplifies growth.

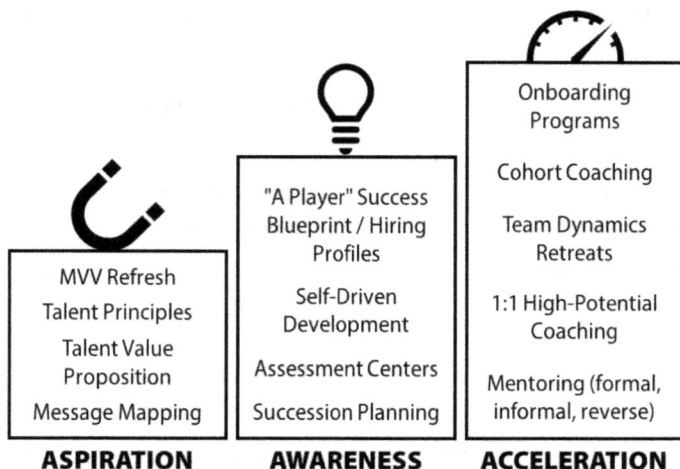

ASPIRATION	AWARENESS	ACCELERATION
MVV Refresh	"A Player" Success Blueprint / Hiring Profiles	Onboarding Programs
Talent Principles		Cohort Coaching
Talent Value Proposition	Self-Driven Development	Team Dynamics Retreats
Message Mapping	Assessment Centers	1:1 High-Potential Coaching
	Succession Planning	Mentoring (formal, informal, reverse)

Powerful questions

Below are some questions to ask yourself, your colleagues, and your employees, that will accelerate trust and cultural cohesion:

- What's the biggest challenge in your role today?

- What's one thing that would make your job easier?

- What is one role in the company you are curious to learn more about?

- Who is one person in a different division / team / location you would love the chance to work with more closely?

- Why did you join the company? Why do you stay?

Key takeaways

1. Trust in leadership is crucial for effective collaboration and problem solving within teams. Violating trust erodes the willingness of employees to share ideas and try new things. Leaders must demonstrate consistency between expectations and actions to instill, inspire, earn, and maintain trust.

2. Low employee engagement has significant consequences, including lower productivity and profitability, higher absenteeism and turnover, and more safety incidents, theft, and quality defects.

3. Leaders can incentivize collaboration by recognizing and rewarding teamwork, breaking down silos, and motivating employees to think and act horizontally. Encouraging entrepreneurial spirit means supporting employees when they try new ideas, even if they fail.

4. Accelerating trust involves being authentic as leaders, fostering collaboration, and creating an environment where people support each other across teams.

5. Understanding individuals' fast lanes, motivations, and communication preferences reduces conflict, improves collaboration, and boosts productivity within teams. Leaders should create an environment where individuals can work and communicate in productive and positive ways.

6. Leaders can accelerate trust by fostering a sense of purpose and helping employees understand the impact of their work on the company's shared mission. Sharing personal motivations and challenges shows vulnerability and builds trust, enabling open and honest dialogue.

7. Cultural cohesion is the ideal outcome of any organization. It is achieved when employees trust each other and their leaders, are incentivized to collaborate not compete, and work together to overcome the organization's biggest hurdles.

Time to apply

1. Review your Acceleration score within your Growth on Purpose assessment scorecard. Commit to taking one action to improve your score within this pillar.

2. During a team-wide meeting, discuss the importance of trust and cohesion. Talk about the benefits of a high-trust culture, and how it can lead to increased engagement, productivity, and innovation. Encourage employees to share their ideas for how to build trust and cohesion within the team.

3. Create a system for incentivizing collaboration and teamwork. This could involve setting team goals, creating cross-functional teams, or implementing a peer recognition program. Reward employees for working together and achieving shared (horizontal) goals, rather than for individual (vertical) achievements only.

4. Empower employees to make decisions and take action. Give them the authority and resources they need to do their jobs effectively, and don't micromanage them. This way, employees will feel more invested in their work and more connected to the team.

5. Hold yourself and other leaders accountable for demonstrating the behaviors you want to see repeated throughout your organization. These include being honest and transparent, fair and consistent, and seeking and acting on feedback. Model the right behaviors to shape a stronger organizational culture.

6. Celebrate successes and recognize the contributions of all stakeholders. Hold regular

team meetings to highlight accomplishments, send out company-wide emails or announcements, or give out awards and bonuses. When employees feel appreciated, they are more likely to be engaged and motivated.

7. What's one hard thing you have been avoiding? Tackle it head on.

SIX

Alignment On What Matters

In building the final pillar, Alignment, you plot the trajectory that will achieve your growth outcomes through greater focus, commitment, and precision; you harness the right ideas, energies, and talents toward pursuit and fulfillment of your purpose.

If you're a fan of 1960s sitcoms, you might remember—or have caught reruns of—a show called *Gilligan's Island*. It told the story of seven people who boarded a tiny boat for a three-hour tour, struck a rock, and became shipwrecked on a deserted island. (Some characters managed to have such an extensive wardrobe that they never wore the same outfit twice in the three years the show ran, but I digress.)

During one episode, a crate of vegetable seeds washed ashore. The castaways were excited to eat veggies again but failed to notice that the crate was labeled "radioactive." Each castaway developed superhuman abilities, such as incredible eyesight, strength, and speed. (Don't worry, the professor eventually made them eat some homemade soap, and everyone recovered. Got to love that guy's ingenuity.)

Neither the magic pill that promises to create limitless performance, nor the magic sugar beets, actually exist. No amount of magic seeds will speed up your growth strategy. But a lot of what you're doing—and not doing—will continue to slow it down.

Why isn't your organization growing as fast as your strategy forecasted?

Powerful connections

Leadership Principle 7:
Leaders make powerful connections

As a leader, it's your job to connect three powerful whys:

1. Your why: Why you do what you do; your personal motivation.

2. Your team's why: Why they show up to work every day; what they are deeply passionate about and what inspires them.

3. Your organization's why: Why your organization exists; its purpose.

When you align all three whys, you ignite a powerful force that can drive perpetual growth. The best and easiest way to build alignment is by making tangible connections between what your people do and why it matters to your shared mission. When people understand how their work contributes to the bigger picture, they are more likely to be engaged and motivated. They are also more likely to stay with the company and contribute to its long-term success.

You can make tangible connections by:

- Sharing stories and examples of how individual and team contributions have made a difference

- Setting clear goals and objectives that are aligned with the organization's why

- Providing regular feedback and recognition for work that is aligned with the whys

This chapter is all about connecting and aligning the three whys. By making tangible connections and by actively and deeply listening to your people, you will create a more engaged and productive workforce.

The "before" state: Low IHR

If you haven't been investing time and energy into stabilizing your Aspiration, Awareness, and Acceleration pillars, then your people won't believe in your mission, won't see where they belong in your culture, and won't understand where and how to contribute. If you have not been nurturing the right talent along the way, your ability to promote from within—your internal hire rate (IHR)—will be significantly hindered. Low IHR causes big cracks in your talent pipeline. Your pipeline will continue to leak because you haven't given your people a reason to grow themselves, their career, or your business. You haven't made the connection for them.

Connect the dots

There are a number of reasons why your people may not feel a strong connection between their individual role and the impact they can have on the company. Here are a few of the most common:

- **Lack of clarity and communication:** If your people don't understand what you're asking of them, or why it's important, it's hard for them to feel engaged and motivated. This is especially true if you're constantly making tactical course corrections, which can make your employees feel like they're chasing a moving target.

- **Lack of alignment between individual and team goals:** If your employees' individual goals are not aligned with the team's goals, they're unlikely to see how their work contributes to the bigger picture.

- **Lack of recognition and reward:** When your employees don't feel recognized or rewarded for their work, they won't feel motivated to go above and beyond.

- **Lack of opportunities for growth and development:** If your employees don't see opportunities for growth and development within the company, they're less likely to be invested in their long-term success.

When your people feel disconnected, it stunts growth in every area of your business:

- **Reduced employee growth:** If your employees can't see how their work contributes to the bigger picture, they won't be motivated to grow and develop.

- **Reduced career growth:** If your employees don't see opportunities for career growth within the company, they're less likely to stay with you for the long term.

- **Reduced business growth:** If your employees are not engaged and motivated, they are less productive… and your business is less profitable.

Stop the "wishy-washy" decision-making

When you're constantly making tactical course corrections, you signal to your employees that you're not sure of what you're doing. This can make them feel like they're working for a leader who is indecisive and wishy-washy.

In addition to eroding trust (see the previous chapter), your indecision has a number of other negative consequences, including:

- **Reduced employee engagement and motivation:** When employees don't feel like they're working toward a clear goal, they're less engaged and motivated.

- **Reduced customer satisfaction:** When employees are not engaged and motivated, they neglect your customers and don't give them the level of service they deserve.

- **Increased employee turnover:** When employees feel like they're working for a tentative leader, they're more likely to look for jobs elsewhere.

If you truly believe that your people are your most valuable asset, you need to invest in them. If you want them to succeed, you need to give them a reason to grow. When you don't, you set your business up for succession gaps in key positions. Those gaps can cripple your business.

What your leaky pipeline is costing you

According to HCMI, external hires come at an 18% higher cost and are 21% more likely to leave within their first year than internal hires. This is because external hires need to be offered higher salaries to entice them to leave their current job and join your company. They also need to be trained in your company's policies and procedures, which takes time and money.

The lottery ticket that created a succession crisis

Several years ago, I was working with an environmental services company, and an employee at one of the job sites hit the lottery. He won $10 million on a scratch-off ticket. Life-changing money. The next day, he rented a limo to drive him to two destinations.

First, to the store that had sold him the winning ticket, so he could buy the store owner a scratch-off ticket to show his appreciation. (He bought one for his limo driver too.)

Second, to his job site, where he promptly resigned.

This employee was a key contributor whose sudden departure left the employer scrambling to replace him.

If you were that lottery winner, how much time would you spend worrying about your company's ability to replace you?

As an employer, how prepared would you be if one of your critical position holders won the lottery? Let's press on this bruise for a moment. What if that critical position holder was also one of your A players? What if several of your critical position holders and A players left tomorrow?

Think no one in your organization is irreplaceable?

Then I have two words for you: Peyton Manning.

Manning's season-ending injury in 2011 shone a light on the fact that the Indianapolis Colts had a backup quarterback who wasn't groomed and wasn't ready. The Colts then went 2-14 that season—the same year their city hosted the Super Bowl. If they wanted to go to the Super Bowl that year, they had to buy tickets just like everybody else.

It wasn't Peyton Manning's job to identify his successor. It was his job to focus on being an A player.

The job of making sure Manning had a viable, ready-now backup belonged to Chris Polian, general manager, and his father, Bill Polian, vice chairman. They didn't pay close enough attention to succession, and they were held accountable for it: Colts owner Jim Irsay fired the father-and-son duo for a string of failures, most notably for not having a good enough talent pipeline.

Let the Indianapolis Colts serve as your cautionary tale. Circumstances happen that knock out your A players. Are you prepared with a pipeline of candidates you've been nurturing, ready to step into each of your key roles?

The Alignment pillar

Alignment is all about making powerful connections for people: Between their individual role and your shared mission; and between the objectives you're asking your team to accomplish and how they move the needle toward your overall business outcomes. Alignment is critical. Because it's too easy to succumb to the daily firefight: To chase all the shiny objects, all the new opportunities, and all the best talent that's available in the market.

If you're not building these pillars in the proper sequence and staying in alignment with where you have committed to grow, it's too easy to fall off the rails. That's a big reason why you lose the right talent, and the best customers, to your competition.

The best method for creating alignment is to set your sights on your long-term horizon, then design every near-term objective, outcome, and decision to move the needle closer to that horizon.

This is also what it takes to go to Mars.

Your Mars mission

In 2022, humans took a significant step toward colonizing Mars, the epitome of an ambitious long-term mission. NASA scientists have concluded that the atmosphere, environment, and potential of Mars make it the most compatible location for a "second Earth"—i.e., a contingency plan for our planet.

Given Earth's distance from Mars—which is always changing, but averages 140 million miles—we can't just decide to go there, design a spaceship, and launch it. It will take a tremendous amount of strategic planning, close collaboration, and tactical execution to get there, as well as a series of carefully planned and executed milestones.

Before we can land on and start to build a colony on Mars, we will need a reliable means of delivering people and supplies so that neither of those invaluable assets becomes damaged. Since the Moon is roughly 1,000 times closer to Earth than Mars is, with many of the same hazards and challenges, scientists will use the Moon as a test environment before embarking on the much longer, more complicated, more dangerous, and more expensive journey to Mars. To create that test environment, astronauts need to travel to the Moon and set up a basecamp where they can live and work for extended periods of time. That's where Artemis I comes in.

Artemis I was the first step in NASA's long-term strategy. Its mission was to send lifelike mannikins to the Moon as a proof of concept. It launched on November 16, 2022 and successfully "splashed down" (returned to Earth) on December 11, 2022.

The next step will be to build the basecamp. And you thought *your* long-term strategy was complex.

Think of your five-year horizon as your "Mars mission." What's the roadmap you need to get there?

There's a well-worn, apocryphal story of the time President John F Kennedy visited NASA, shortly after he announced that the United States would put a man on the Moon before the end of the decade. It was the 1960s, the Age of Camelot, and a time when bold leaders challenged the people around them to do what seemed impossible.

As Kennedy walked the halls of NASA, he came upon a janitor. Being the charismatic young leader he was, Kennedy approached the gentleman and asked, "What is your job here?" As the story goes, the janitor replied, "I'm helping to put a man on the Moon."

Everyone at NASA—from the engineers to the mathematicians, to the people constructing the rocket, to the people identifying and evaluating the would-be explorers of the cosmos, and even the janitor—felt a connection between their individual role and why it mattered to the big, audacious goal. The janitor knew that if he didn't do his job, if he didn't keep his assigned areas of NASA clean and dry, someone could slip and fall, or become ill, and be unable to do *their* job. And if enough people couldn't do their jobs, we never would have succeeded in our Moon mission.

I wasn't around in the 1960s, so I don't know if this story is true. But I like to think it is.

When every member of your team feels a tangible connection between what they do and why it matters, they enthusiastically contribute their best ideas, talents, and efforts—individually and collaboratively—to fulfilling your shared mission.

But your people won't all automatically "get it." As a leader, you must help them make those connections. Once they feel connected, their engagement will increase exponentially. The first step is to break your people free from their silos.

Not one organization I know intentionally forms silos. Yet not one organization I know lacks them. Silos are what keep you from achieving your mission and your growth strategy. They are what hold your people back from communicating and collaborating effectively. And they are what motivate your people to resist growth, stop contributing, and eventually leave. Let's change that by strengthening your Alignment pillar.

What Alignment looks like

Increasing alignment between your talent and your growth strategy is mission-critical. It's also easier than you might think. Here are five actions you can take right now.

1. Leadership summits

Dedicating two days to an off-site summit is never convenient, but it is always a worthwhile investment. If you do not step out of the daily firefight and quarterly financial monitoring of your business, you will never reach the long-term horizon you're aiming for. Commit to bringing together your senior leadership teams. Go beyond merely providing progress reports, and intentionally work to break down silos and align their vertical strategies to achieve your shared vision.

Spend day one on strengthening your team's dynamics—their ability and willingness to work together and support one another. Re-read the Acceleration chapter for simple ways to do that and to adapt my sample agenda.

Day two is all about creating strategic alignment by identifying your Mars mission and then reverse engineering the roadmap that will get you there:

- **Your Mars mission:** What's your long-term growth objective? What outcomes must your business achieve within the next five years? How will you define success?

- **Your sustainable delivery model:** To achieve your long-term strategy, what systems, processes, and infrastructure must you have in place by year four to ensure a reliable delivery of your products and services to your clients and customers… and to ensure a reliable pipeline of the right talent to fulfill that delivery?

- **Your Moon basecamp:** Think of your medium-term operating plan as the basecamp you need to build. What do you need to do over the next two to three years to achieve that mission? Which capabilities and initiatives are mission-critical?

- **Your Artemis I:** Now view your near-term objectives through the lens of the three stages above. What objectives and deliverables must you prioritize over the next six to eighteen months? How do your long-term Mars mission; your need for a reliable delivery system of the right products, services, and talent; and your medium-term basecamp focus those priorities?

If you'd like to see the day two agenda I use in my facilitation, which focuses on creating strategic alignment, you can download it for free at www.growthonpurpose.com / resources.

Visualizing your future success—then intentionally and methodically mapping out the interim milestones and metrics required to achieve it—is essential for making sound decisions, leading your organization to victory, and creating a lasting legacy.

2. Decision dashboard

Bringing together your leadership team for two days each year to build and recalibrate your longer-term strategy is a tremendous first step toward alignment. But many leaders still commit one deadly sin that threatens the momentum such leadership summits create. That sin is indecisiveness.

According to Bain & Company, 92% of private equity firms reported that waiting too long to act on talent issues resulted in their portfolio company underperforming over a five-year holding period.

Whether you're growing through M&A, expanding into a new division or product area, or adding one new hire at a time, the research consistently shows that failing to make timely decisions—particularly those related to talent—leads to lower performance, higher turnover, and greater disengagement. You need to figure out how to make not just talent decisions, but *every* decision, easier, faster, and better. The best way to do that is by developing a decision dashboard.

A decision dashboard enables you to run your business from one sheet of paper, by ensuring that you and your teams make every decision with your longer-term strategy in mind. First, grab the free template at www.growthonpurpose.com/resources. Then, you can quickly create your own decision dashboard:

- **Mission, Vision, and Values:** Unless you've forgotten everything you've read in this book up to this point, you know that your MVV is foundational to your growth journey. Review the Aspiration chapter if you need a refresher. Then write your MVV along the bottom of your dashboard.

- **Mission-Critical DNA:** On the back of your dashboard, make a detailed list of the fundamental capabilities, skills, technical expertise, knowledge, and behaviors you and your team must possess and display to achieve your mission. Make sure to include the DNA of your A players on that list.

Now, using the FLOW chart method identify the following:

- **FUNDAMENTALS:** Looking over that list of mission-critical attributes, which ones are currently lacking or underrepresented in your organization? Those are your fundamental gaps. Write those items in the "Fundamentals" box on your decision dashboard.

- **LEVERS:** Again looking at your mission-critical list, which ones are current strengths within your organization? These are competitive advantages that you and your team can leverage. Write those items in the "Levers" box.

- **OBSTACLES:** What obstacles stand in the way of your ability to achieve your mission? These might include, but would not be limited to, high turnover, low engagement, and low IHR. Write these in the "Obstacles" box.

- **WINS:** What will success look like? How will you know a win when you see it? What milestones must you hit? What quick wins can you implement? Write those in the "Wins" box.

The leaders I work with refer to their one-page decision dashboard daily. They display it in their offices and conference rooms. They carry a copy in their pocket. Whenever they need to make a decision—whether strategic or day-to-day—they measure it against the dashboard and ask, does this decision:

- Address one of our fundamental gaps?

- Leverage one of our competitive strengths?

- Minimize or eliminate an obstacle?

- Achieve or move us closer to a win?

Involve others on your team in the development of your decision dashboard. Refer to it as often as possible. When you convert a fundamental gap into a lever of strength—or an obstacle into an opportunity—be sure to update your dashboard accordingly and celebrate the win with your team. Small wins create big ones.

3. High-potential thinktanks

In 1980, the US Men's Hockey Team won the Olympic Gold medal against incredible odds. They were a team of college-aged athletes who had never played together before—in fact, many of them had been fierce rivals on competing teams.

In building the team, head coach Herb Brooks defied the "experts" and pundits by selecting players who were not necessarily the best individual superstars, but instead possessed the raw DNA that would mesh together most effectively as a team. Brooks understood what his critics didn't: That few experiences bond people faster than the opportunity to fight a common enemy. In the case of the US Men's Hockey Team, one enemy was the formidable Russian team, which was well stocked with veteran professional hockey players who had played together for years. The other enemy was Brooks himself, who was famously ruthless in how he trained, conditioned, and disciplined his players. The more the players hated him (and his dreaded whistle), the less time they had to hate each other.

Don't misunderstand me. I am not advocating that you and your fellow leaders start blowing whistles at work or becoming hard to follow. Instead, give your people a common enemy. And do it in a way that not only increases team cohesion, but also makes your organization more efficient and productive.

Start with your highest-potential talent. Invite them to participate in a full-day "thinktank." (The idea of taking part in a thinktank will boost their engagement before they even walk into the session.) Borrow from the agendas I shared earlier to strengthen their team dynamics and alignment, but as the primary focus of the event, give them a big problem to solve. Do not make the problem an academic one—for example, handing them a business case study you downloaded off the Harvard Business School website. There will be plenty of problems and dysfunctional areas to tackle within your own organization. Here are two ideas to get you started:

- What is the most **pressing problem** plaguing your organization? Have you lost a key client or customer? Has a recent downsizing forced you to accomplish the same outcomes with fewer resources? Have industry forces or market trends changed the way you need to operate? Pick one or more of your most pressing problems; get specific on the nature, extent, and consequences of the problem; and challenge the group to solve it.

- How many **work processes** are both critical to the way you operate and ridiculously cumbersome? Have the group come up with a list of the most frustrating processes throughout the organization, then vote on the process that is both the most critical and the most cumbersome. Using butcher paper or a long whiteboard, have the team map out every single step, component, and decision point in the end-to-end process. Once they're comfortable that the process is completely mapped out, challenge them to re-engineer it. What steps can be consolidated or removed without sacrificing quality or accuracy? Which decision points can happen sooner, with fewer decision-makers, and in less time?

Stop kicking the can down the road, living with problem X and telling yourself that you'll get around to solving it eventually. Create a forum for your high-potential talent, then give them free rein to co-create a solution to the problem. Their fresh perspective, enthusiasm, and innovative approaches might surprise you. While they help you remove a roadblock to your growth, they will also deepen their commitment to your organization—and you will strengthen your talent pipeline.

4. Strategy development and alignment

The fastest way to reduce the shelf life of your business strategy is, ironically, to put it on a shelf. Like your TVP, your succession plans, and your decision dashboard, your business strategy must be a living document that you evaluate regularly—and against which you measure your progress. Hold yourself and your business accountable to the strategy you developed and the Talent Principles you created. Regularly revisit and refresh your business and people strategies to ensure not only that they stay aligned, but that you have a well-designed roadmap for fulfilling them.

Your annual leadership summit, followed by at least annual (but ideally quarterly) follow-up sessions, are great forums for pressure-testing your strategy and ensuring that it remains relevant and on course.

5. Talent plan and narrative

When you complete the actions within this book, you will generate a tremendous amount of momentum. By bringing in the right talent, nurturing them, and providing opportunities for them to give input into your growth journey, you will increase buy-in and deepen commitment.

Don't stop there.

Craft a compelling talent plan and narrative that provide the business rationale for investing in the right talent, over the long term, to ensure the sustainable growth of your business. Make sure your narrative presents such an elegant solution to your low attraction, retention, engagement, and IHR, that your stakeholders can't wait to invest in it... and in you. Then use that narrative to influence every roadshow, town hall, corporate communication, and HR initiative. It's imperative that you and your fellow leaders recognize and communicate the inextricable link between your business plan and your talent strategy. When you speak with conviction about your strategy—instead of trying to "convince" people that this is the right path—you will inspire every key stakeholder to understand, believe in, and buy into their role in fulfilling it.

The growth of your business is a journey. Invite everyone in your organization to take part in it.

Scaling a business without increasing overhead

The owner of a single-location business in the hospitality industry was struggling to grow his business. He had ninety employees and a ten-person senior leadership team. He wanted to double his revenue within eighteen months without doubling his overhead.

The problem was that his team wasn't ready to scale. The frontline workers were young and didn't see any career growth potential, so they had a high turnover rate. The organizational culture was strong, but the team didn't have the processes and infrastructure in place to support rapid growth.

The business owner knew that he needed to make some changes if he wanted to achieve his goals, so he brought me in to assess and accelerate his business's growth readiness.

Over the next ninety days, I worked with the owner and his leadership team to:

- Map out their mission and growth ambitions

- Compile an inventory of fundamental capabilities and mission-critical roles required to achieve them
- Measure the current state of their team and business
- Inventory and address key fundamental gaps and existing strengths
- Identify the top flight risks on the leadership team and develop recommendations for retaining them and increasing their engagement
- Build a one-page decision dashboard to enable them to make near-term and long-term business decisions easier, faster, and better
- Develop the Growth on Purpose roadmap to scale with clarity and confidence

By the end of the ninety-day engagement, the business owner had a clear understanding of his team's strengths and weaknesses, as well as the key gaps they needed to fill in order to scale successfully. He also had a comprehensive roadmap for implementing the necessary changes.

The business owner immediately began implementing the Growth on Purpose roadmap. He invested in training and development programs for his frontline workers, and he created new career paths so that they could see a future for themselves at the company. He also implemented new systems and processes to streamline operations and improve efficiency.

As a result of these changes, the business owner was able to achieve his growth goals ahead of schedule. He doubled the number of locations within eighteen months, and he continues to grow his business today.

He told me, "We are now poised for greater success in growing the individuals on our team beyond their own dreams and serving the community as a whole with greater purpose."

His head of operations added, "This is a remarkable process with a highly actionable roadmap toward ensuring our readiness to grow."

The "ideal" state: Strategic fulfillment

The Alignment pillar is the culmination of the three pillars that precede it. It's the end zone. The only way your business can win is through fulfillment of your growth strategy in a predictable and repeatable way. To reach strategic fulfillment, convene summits in which your senior leaders break down vertical silos and align horizontally; use a one-page decision dashboard to view every business decision through your Aspirational lens; bring together your high-potential talent to solve your most pressing business problems; regularly recalibrate your business strategy; and share a talent narrative that brings that business strategy to life.

Strategic fulfillment is the ideal outcome of a business that is crystal clear on its aspirations, keenly aware of its strengths and blind spots, accelerates trust by demonstrating transparency and removing obstacles to collaboration, and deeply and powerfully aligns the work its people do with how it impacts the shared mission, vision, and values. When you achieve strategic fulfillment, you generate dependable continuity. By giving people a reason to grow, you will create a talent pipeline that nourishes itself and fuels your perpetual growth engine.

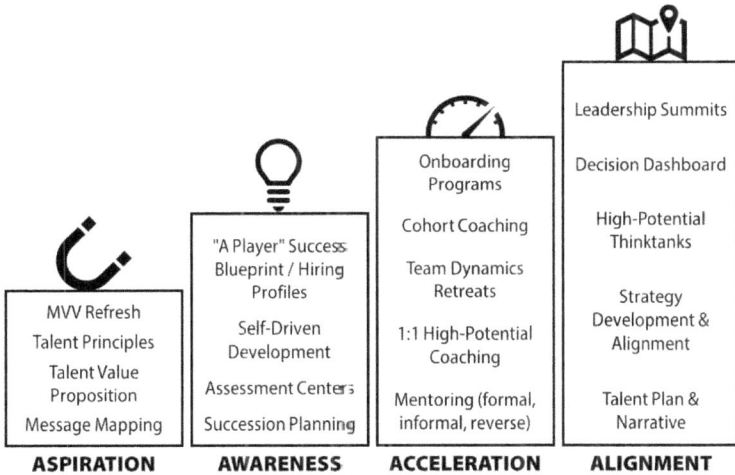

ASPIRATION	AWARENESS	ACCELERATION	ALIGNMENT
MVV Refresh	"A Player" Success Blueprint / Hiring Profiles	Onboarding Programs	Leadership Summits
Talent Principles	Self-Driven Development	Cohort Coaching	Decision Dashboard
Talent Value Proposition	Assessment Centers	Team Dynamics Retreats	High-Potential Thinktanks
Message Mapping	Succession Planning	1:1 High-Potential Coaching	Strategy Development & Alignment
		Mentoring (formal, informal, reverse)	Talent Plan & Narrative

Powerful questions

Below are some questions to ask yourself, your colleagues, and your employees, that will increase alignment and strategic fulfillment:

- Why does your role exist? What is it intended to accomplish?

- What do you get to do in your role that others may not know about?

139

- How does your individual role contribute to our shared mission?

- What is the most cumbersome process you have to navigate to get work done? What would make that process simpler?

Key takeaways

1. Leaders play a crucial role in connecting three significant "whys": personal motivation (your why), team passion (your team's why), and organizational purpose (organizational why). Aligning these creates a powerful force that drives perpetual growth.

2. Building alignment involves making tangible connections between individual and team contributions and the organization's mission. This includes sharing stories of impact, setting clear goals, and providing regular feedback and recognition aligned with the three whys.

3. A lack of investment in stabilizing the Aspiration, Awareness, and Acceleration pillars can result in a low IHR. This leads to leaks in your talent pipeline and hinders your long-term success and growth.

4. Indecisiveness and constant tactical course corrections can erode trust, reduce employee engagement, increase turnover, and negatively

affect customer satisfaction. Strong connections between individual roles and overall impact are crucially important for employee, career, and business growth.

5. The Alignment pillar enables strategic fulfillment. It involves actions such as leadership summits, decision dashboards, high-potential thinktanks, strategy development, and a compelling talent narrative. Achieving strategic fulfillment creates dependable continuity and a self-nourishing talent pipeline for perpetual growth.

Time to apply

1. Review your Alignment score within your Growth on Purpose assessment scorecard. Commit to taking one action to improve your score within this pillar.

2. Capture the three whys, then share these with your team.

   - Your why: Write down your personal *why* statement. Why do you do what you do? Why does it matter to you?

   - Your team's why: Bring together your team and ask them to write down their individual why statements. Then, as a team, identify the common themes and values that emerge.

- Your organization's why: Capture your organization's why statement, which is its purpose for existing.

3. Make tangible connections between what your people do and why it matters to your shared mission.

   - Share stories and examples of how individual and team contributions have made a difference. This could be done through team meetings, company newsletters, or social media.

   - Set clear goals and objectives that are aligned with the organization's why. Make sure everyone in the organization understands the goals and objectives, and how their work contributes to achieving them.

   - Provide regular feedback and recognition for work that is aligned with the three whys. This will help to motivate employees and show them that their work is valued.

4. Implement quick wins and celebrate longer-term victories.

   - Identify a few small wins that can be achieved quickly, for example improving customer satisfaction or reducing costs.

   - Celebrate these wins with your team to boost morale and motivation.

- Set longer-term goals and objectives, such
  as increasing market share or launching a
  new product.

- Regularly recognize and reward employees
  for their contributions to achieving the
  longer-term goals.

5. Take one action *today* to make a more powerful
   connection between your employees' individual
   efforts and your shared mission.

SEVEN

Time To Grow

Now that we've walked through the entire Growth on Purpose model, you understand that seeding your organization with the right talent leads to perpetual growth.

Leadership Principle 8:
Leaders grow on purpose

Leaders must strategize, synthesize, motivate, and act. And they must lead from the front. Get ready to create a growth journey so magnetic that the right talent wants to join, stay, contribute, and grow.

Culture matters: Measure it, then move it

If you had any doubts before reading this book, I hope you now deeply understand that *culture matters*. Culture is foundational to the success of your business. And not only is it possible to measure culture, it is *imperative* if you are to have any chance of transforming it into a platform for perpetual growth.

As we explored in Chapter One, the strength of your culture—and consequently, the reliability of your business growth—is measured by four key indicators. To recap:

1. **Attraction rate:** Is the right talent joining? When the right people don't believe in your mission and vision, and when they hear through others that your actual culture doesn't deliver what your employer brand promises, they won't apply to your organization. And while it takes more time, effort, and investment to pull the right people into your orbit, hiring the wrong-fit talent will cost you more. You need to give the right people a reason to *join*.

2. **Retention rate:** Is your talent staying? When your best talent sprints for the exits, they leave behind the wrong-fit talent, conflict, and presenteeism. The right talent is expensive to replace, so you need to give those people a reason to *stay*.

3. **Engagement rate:** Is your talent contributing? Culture clashes and change resistance can leave you and your teams disillusioned and unmotivated. Low engagement harms your productivity and profitability, so you need to give people a reason to *contribute*.

4. **Internal hire rate:** Is your talent growing? If you're unable to show clear career paths, you will create succession and talent gaps, driving up the cost to fill mission-critical positions. Remember, external hires are more expensive and more likely to leave within their first year, so you need to give people a reason to *grow* within your organization.

The lower your ability to attract, retain, engage, and advance the right talent, the more money your business will lose... and the sooner your growth engine will grind to a halt.

Before you can fire up that growth engine, you must stop building silos and start bringing together the 4Ps of culture. To remind you, the 4Ps are:

1. **People:** Your *who*. You must have the right people in the right roles, with the right skills and motivation.

2. **Process:** Your *how*. You must have systems and methods that replicate your best practices and engineer out inefficiencies.

3. **Performance:** Your *what*. You must have outcomes that move the needle on your business strategy, in ways that demonstrate the behaviors you want to see repeated.

4. **Purpose:** Your *why*, which resides at the intersection of the other three Ps. You must have a magnetic mission and vision that the right talent cannot wait to help you fulfill.

The four pillars

With purpose as your sweet spot, you can implement the four pillars of the Growth on Purpose model—a tangible, actionable method for achieving perpetual growth. Let's briefly recap what we've learned in the last four chapters to summarize the essence of the model.

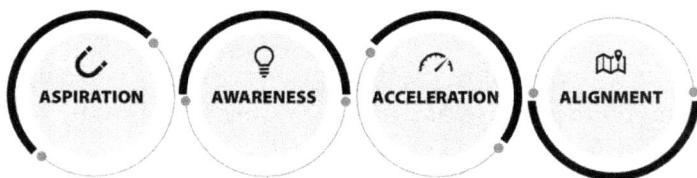

Aspiration

Use your magnetic *why* to attract, retain, and inspire more of the right people. Design a mission that pushes you, a vision that pulls you, and values that keep you on course. Then create a set of Talent Principles that hold every leader accountable to nurturing talent in the right direction, a compelling TVP that promises a brand that your culture actually delivers, and a message map that ensures everyone communicates in a consistent and compelling way to all stakeholders in and around your business. The ideal state of this pillar is **magnetic purpose**, which, when you have it, attracts the right talent to your door, pre-sold on joining your cause.

Awareness

Replicate your best performers and create fast lanes to turn potential into performance. Tap into what makes your A players so effective and put as many people as possible in the best position to succeed. While you use your A player DNA profile to find and build more of the right talent, you must provide all employees with self-driven development opportunities, run assessment centers to identify and evolve your raw talent, and strengthen the line of succession for your A players and critical position holders. The ideal state of this pillar is **limitless talent**, where the right talent stays longer, and their engagement, productivity, and fulfillment create innovative breakthroughs, competitive advantage, and year-over-year profitability.

Acceleration

Increase trust in leadership and strengthen team dynamics to solve bigger problems faster. Deepen collaboration and chemistry across teams so you can tackle the biggest roadblocks along your growth journey. Then create onboarding programs that increase commitment, start developing your high potentials earlier, raise the minimum proficiency of all people managers, and encourage—and simplify—mentoring in all directions. The ideal state of this pillar is **cultural cohesion**, where every member of your team feels connected to each other, enthusiastically supports one another's success, and contributes their best talents and ideas to your shared mission.

Alignment

Plot the trajectory that achieves your growth outcomes with focus, commitment, and precision. Bring your leadership together more often—not to fixate on last quarter's progress, but to envision your long-term horizon, and to map out the steps and milestones required to get there. Then build a dashboard that helps you make better, faster, easier decisions; empower and challenge your rising talent to solve the biggest obstacles along your growth path; re-examine and recalibrate your strategy to maintain alignment; and tell a talent story that you and everyone around you can deeply believe in and bring to life. The ideal state of this pillar is **strategic fulfillment**, where every employee feels such a tangible, powerful connection between what they do and why it matters that they actively—and with deep conviction—grow themselves, their careers, and your business. In turn, you create a talent pipeline that nourishes itself.

The right components in the right order

When you implement the four pillars of the Growth on Purpose model, in the sequence outlined in this book, you will give the right talent a reason to join, stay, contribute, and grow. You will attract the right people to your magnetic purpose. You will create fast lanes that unlock limitless talent and combine that talent in ways that strengthen cultural cohesion. And you will powerfully connect your talent to your strategy, so you can fuel your perpetual growth.

If you've been struggling to get these results on your own, you're likely missing a few of these key components or are simply trying to put them together in the wrong order. Work your way through the list below to check that you have all the fundamental building blocks in place:

1. Light the way with a clear **Aspiration**. What is your company's magnetic why? What is the mission that pushes you and the vision that pulls you? What values keep you on the right path?

Once you have a clear aspiration, you can articulate it to your team and start attracting the right talent to join your journey. Remember that your entire ecosystem starts with introducing the *right* talent into your culture. Give new talent a reason to believe and existing talent a reason to belong.

2. Feed your passion and that of your people through **Awareness** of self. Tap into the genius of your employees and empower them to drive their own development. Help them to understand their strengths, weaknesses, and motivations. When your employees are keenly aware of their strengths, they can operate in their fast lanes and contribute in more meaningful ways.

3. Do the hard things that enable **Acceleration** of trust. This means being transparent, removing obstacles to collaboration, and demonstrating that you care about your people's wellbeing and your team's success. When your employees trust you, they are more likely to stay with your company and contribute at their highest level.

4. Make powerful connections that foster **Alignment** of your talent with what matters to your business. This means helping your employees understand how their individual roles contribute to defeating a common enemy and fulfilling a shared mission. It also means creating a culture where everyone feels connected to each other and to the company's success.

The result

When you clarify your purpose, you galvanize your culture. That's the key to multiplying the value of your business and to Growth on Purpose. Remember that when you get the right talent to *join* your business and give them a reason to *stay*, they will want to *contribute*. The more they contribute, the more they—and your business—will *grow*. The more they grow, the longer they will stay and the more likely they are to tell their friends about their experience, which will in turn entice more of the right people to join and begin the cycle again.

The four pillars that drive your Growth on Purpose yield enormous payoffs for your people, your business, and your legacy:

- **Differentiated culture:** By giving people a reason to *join*, you will entice and invite the right talent to enthusiastically want to work for you.

- **Driven commitment:** By giving your people a reason to *stay*, you will have more of the right talent in place to fulfill your purpose.

- **Deep connection:** By giving people a reason to *contribute*, you will have a strong, fit, integrated culture that amplifies growth.

- **Dependable continuity:** By giving people a reason to *grow*, you will have a talent pipeline that nourishes itself.

I've been cancer-free since 2011. But I still get regular testing and scans to make sure the cancer doesn't return or lead to what doctors call "structural disease." You must do the same for your business. Make sure you regularly reassess the health of your organization—its structural soundness—to ensure you're not eroding your effectiveness.

Growth on Purpose is cyclical, not linear. When you are crystal clear on your *aspiration* for your business, you are keenly *aware* of your strengths and blind spots, you *accelerate* trust by demonstrating transparency and removing obstacles to your team's ability to collaborate, and you deeply and powerfully *align* the work your people do with how it impacts the longer-term mission, you will achieve strategic fulfillment. In this state, you will see perpetual growth, because you have crafted an irresistibly magnetic purpose, removed obstacles to unlock limitless talent and enable cultural cohesion, and harnessed those resources toward achieving a shared goal that everyone cares deeply about. It's a cycle you can replicate to fulfill your growth strategy and multiply your success.

The full talent ecosystem

Growing on purpose is not easy, but it is essential for businesses that want to thrive in today's competitive marketplace. By installing the four pillars of Growth on Purpose, you will create a full talent ecosystem and differentiated culture that attract and retain top talent, drive innovation, and deliver perpetual growth. By investing in your people and your culture, you will create a business that is poised for success in the years to come. The future is bright for leaders who are committed to growing on purpose.

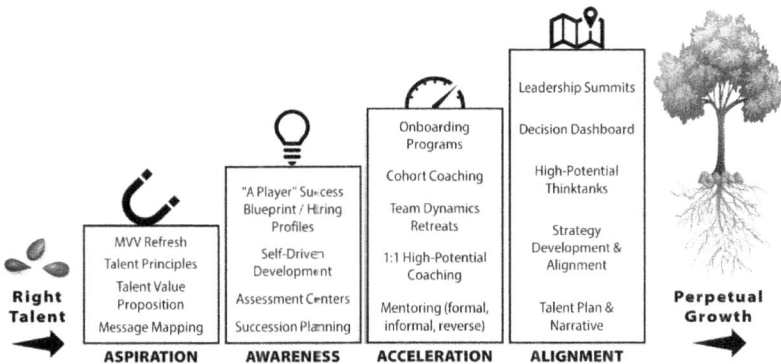

ASPIRATION	AWARENESS	ACCELERATION	ALIGNMENT
MVV Refresh	"A Player" Success Blueprint / Hiring Profiles	Onboarding Programs	Leadership Summits
Talent Principles	Self-Driven Development	Cohort Coaching	Decision Dashboard
Talent Value Proposition	Assessment Centers	Team Dynamics Retreats	High-Potential Thinktanks
Message Mapping	Succession Planning	1:1 High-Potential Coaching	Strategy Development & Alignment
		Mentoring (formal, informal, reverse)	Talent Plan & Narrative

Right Talent → ... → Perpetual Growth

If you'd like a full-sized version of the talent ecosystem, you can download it at www.growthonpurpose.com/resources.

What next?

Growth on Purpose is simpler than you might believe. You are one decision, one step, one action away from applying this model to your business and gaining immediate value. But if it still seems daunting, here are some next steps you can take.

Create capacity

The most difficult part of the Growth on Purpose model is finding time to implement it. You need to create the capacity to take action, so open up your calendar. For each recurring meeting, ask yourself:

- Does it need to run this long?

- Does it need to occur this often?

- Do I need to be in it?

Remove yourself from as many meetings as possible. The only reason you should be in a recurring meeting is to reach key decisions, solve problems, or embed best practices. If others can run the meeting without you, let them. If the meeting would be just as productive if it happened less often or was shorter in duration, scale it back.

You will be amazed by how much time you can gain by decluttering your calendar. Once you have created that space, do not fill it with more meetings. Block out the time and use it strategically: To engage in long-term planning, to check in with key stakeholders, or simply to think. And, of course, to apply the Growth on Purpose model.

Every spring, I clean out my closet. Sometimes, I need a little help from someone who isn't emotionally attached to my sh—stuff. So I call my best friend, who will ruthlessly weed out every article of clothing that doesn't fit, is out of style, or flat out doesn't suit me. If you need help decluttering your calendar, grab fifteen minutes on *my* calendar and we'll identify at least three items you can remove, reduce, or recycle from yours: www.growthonpurpose.com/calendar.

Test drive the diagnostic tools

As I mentioned earlier in this book, an integral part of my client advisory work is a suite of battle-tested, science-backed, and EEO-compliant diagnostic tools. It's important to work out which tools will be right for you. Before you go "all in" on assessments, try them out to get a better understanding of how they work and how you can best leverage them to accelerate growth.

Visit this link to test drive one of the diagnostic tools I use: www.growthonpurpose.com/insights.

Set your next milestones

Earlier in the book, I challenged you to benchmark your current performance by completing the Growth on Purpose assessment. It's free and takes about five minutes: www.growthonpurpose.com/assessment.

Once you complete the assessment, you'll receive a personalized report that recommends where to focus your efforts first. Use that input to identify your near-term milestones.

Rather than trying to figure out how to take your business performance from its current state to best-in-class overnight, take it one step at a time. Think back to the concept of the Mars mission: If best-in-class is your longer-term goal, how can you reverse-engineer your path to get there? Where do your scores need to be within the next four years? The next two to three years? The next six to eighteen months? Plant your flag, challenge your team, and remove the obstacles standing between you and those milestones. Don't forget to celebrate your small wins along the way.

Decide your leadership principles

Reflect on the leadership principles provided in this book and identify which speak loudest to you:

1. Leaders own their walk.

2. Leaders shape culture.

3. Leaders multiply value.

4. Leaders light the way.

5. Leaders feed their passion.

6. Leaders do hard things.

7. Leaders make powerful connections.

8. Leaders grow on purpose.

Key takeaways

1. Culture is the key to business success. It is essential to measure culture (attraction rate, retention rate, engagement rate, and internal hire rate) so that you can harness it for perpetual growth.

2. Work on your pillars in the right order to build on your successes and ensure optimal results.

3. The payoffs of successful implementation of the Growth on Purpose model are differentiated culture, driven commitment, deep connection, and dependable continuity.

4. If you truly want to drive Growth on Purpose within your organization and achieve perpetual growth, you need to do four things well: create and consistently express a magnetic purpose; unleash limitless talent; strengthen cultural cohesion; and facilitate strategic fulfillment.

Time to apply

1. Make a list of your own leadership principles. Share them with your team. Live them every day.

2. Audit your calendar—what meetings can you lose, or remove yourself from, to make time and space to focus on your Growth on Purpose journey?

3. Choose one diagnostic tool to test drive this week.

4. Decide what you want your Growth on Purpose assessment scores to be in one, two, and three years' time.

5. What's one action you will take today to grow on purpose?

Conclusion

In the fall of 2011, my cancer surgery was behind me, but I still had a lifetime of follow-up lab work, scans, and doctor's check-ins ahead of me. I returned to the hospital one day for my latest blood draw. I checked in at the front desk, showed my identification, proof of insurance, and method of payment, and then waited for my turn with the phlebotomist. When my name was called, I stood up, walked to booth three, and said a silent prayer that the needle would find the vein without any trouble. I had a smooth stick (whew), filled a vial or two, got my bandage, and headed out.

As I was walking toward the exit, a woman in the waiting room stopped me.

"I just have to tell you," she told me, "You have the happiest walk I've ever seen. It made my day."

That's why I never tone down my walk. And it's why you shouldn't either. You never know who's watching, and what impact you can have on them, so *own your walk.*

Succeeding in implementing the Growth on Purpose model will open doorways to greater challenges. At the beginning of this book, I told you that I've got you. During the hardest day of my life, my friend called to give me that same message. That's exactly what your employees need to hear, feel, and believe: That you as an organization have their back, have thoughtfully crafted a path for them where they can contribute their best talents and ideas to a mission that aligns with their passions, and have intentionally nurtured a culture in which failing forward leads to breakthroughs.

When you apply the leadership principles and the Growth on Purpose model, you will finally be able to tell your employees, "We've got you."

And they will finally believe you.

90-Day Growth on Purpose Strategy Intensive

If you have ambitious growth goals over the next three years—and you're not convinced you have the internal horsepower to achieve them—don't build your strategy on your own.

The 90-day Growth on Purpose Strategy Intensive will rigorously evaluate the current state of your talent, their degree of alignment with your growth strategy, and their capacity to achieve it. Imagine, 90 days from now, having a clear roadmap for addressing your biggest gaps and propelling your growth strategy.

To learn more about the Strategy Intensive and find out whether it's the right fit for your organization, visit www.growthonpurpose.com/strategy.

Final Thoughts

I'm here today because of Sunday dinners.

Growing up, my brother and I played sports and had other after-school activities, but never to the "every-minute-is-calendared" degree of some kids today. We knew homework had to be done before the TV could go on. We knew that when the streetlights kicked on, that was our cue to return home from playing down the block. We knew that the perfect summer day started in our friend's backyard pool, continued with kickball in the street, and ended with a rousing game of Ghosts in the Graveyard. We knew that Sunday mornings were for Church, and that Sunday dinners were for family. Even after my brother and I each moved out on our own, we returned for Sunday dinners.

One Sunday in 1997, I was at my parents' house. Mom had kicked us out of the kitchen, so my dad, my brother and I were watching TV in the den, various sections of the Sunday newspaper spread out in front of us. I had been the last to arrive for dinner, so the only section left unclaimed was the classifieds. As I flipped through the oversized pages—not really reading, since I wasn't actively job-hunting, but buying time until the comics section became available—an ad caught my eye. It was for a manager of a small marketing production team at a company I was unfamiliar with, headquartered in a New Jersey town I had never heard of. But it spoke to me. The ad described the job I was already in, plus the promise of more. More challenge. More opportunity. More impact.

I tore the ad from the paper, stuffed it into my pocket and helped Mom set the table for dinner. Later that week, I uncrumpled the ad, wrote a cover letter expressing my interest in the position, and mailed it along with a copy of my resume to the company. (This was in the "old days", before online applications.) It took over a month to hear back. (Yes, HR was slow to respond even then.) But ultimately, I got an interview, then another, and eventually I got the job.

If I hadn't gotten that job offer, I wouldn't have left the company and the job I had been in since college. I wouldn't have had the chance to work for the best and worst executive leaders in my career. I wouldn't have had the opportunity to change careers multiple times within the same company. I wouldn't have acquired the expertise and perspective that those various roles provided me. And when I was diagnosed with cancer, I wouldn't have had the motivation to leap into the entrepreneurial unknown. Oh—and I wouldn't have met and married my husband.

If not for Sunday dinners, I wouldn't have crossed paths with the opportunity that ultimately led me here: Through a corporate career and into an entrepreneurial journey that has enabled me to do work I love, with people I deeply care about, in ways that fuel their business and feed my passion.

Why are *you* here?

Where will it lead you?

References

Allen, David G. *Retaining Talent: A guide to analyzing and managing employee turnover*. SHRM Foundation's Effective Practice Guidelines Series, 2008.

Aon Hewitt. *Culture Integration in M&A: Survey findings*. 2011. www.aon.com/attachments/thought-leadership/M_A_Survey.pdf

Bain & Company. *Global Private Equity Report*. 2021. www.bain.com/globalassets/noindex/2021/bain_report_2021-global-private-equity-report.pdf

Brown, Brené. *Atlas of the Heart: Mapping meaningful connection and the language of Human Experience*. Random House, 2021.

Brown, Brené. *Dare To Lead: Brave work. Tough conversations. Whole hearts*. Random House, 2018.

Business Wire. "Oscar Mayer Takes Hot Dogs to New Heights with Latest WienerFleet Addition, the JetPack-Powered Super Hotdogger." June 18, 2018. https://ir.kraftheinzcompany.com/news-releases/news-release-details/oscar-mayer-takes-hot-dogs-new-heights-latest-wienerfleet

Connors, Roger, and Tom Smith. *Change the Culture, Change the Game: The breakthrough strategy for energizing your organization and creating accountability for results.* Penguin Group, 2011.

Damodaran, Aswath. *The Little Book of Valuation: How to value a company, pick a stock and profit.* Wiley, 2011.

Doyle, Glennon. *Untamed: Stop pleasing, start living.* Vermilion, 2020.

ESPN. "Peyton Manning: Firing 'very tough'." January 2, 2012. www.espn.com/nfl/story/_/id/7414912/polians-relieved-duties-indianapolis-colts-source-says

Gallup. "The Benefits of Employee Engagement." Updated: January 7, 2023. www.gallup.com/workplace/236927/employee-engagement-drives-growth.aspx

Glazer, Robert. "'Command and Control' Leadership Is Dead. Here's What's Taking Its Place." *Inc. Magazine*, August 12, 2019. www.inc.com/robert-glazer/command-control-leadership-is-dead-heres-whats-taking-its-place.html

Hartman, Robert S. *The Structure of Value: Foundations of scientific axiology.* Wipf & Stock, 2011.

Human Capital Management Institute (HCMI). "Internal Hire Rate: What It Is, Why Use It, and How to Calculate It." Updated: March 27, 2023. www. hcmi.co/post/internal-hire-rate

Huntsinger, Gina. "A celebration of football in Peanuts coincides with Super Bowl 50." Charles M. Schulz Museum and Research Center, January 5, 2016. https://schulzmuseum.org/wp-content/uploads/2016/01/Its-a-Foul-Its-a-Field-Goal-It s-Football-News-Release.pdf

IMDb. Gilligan's Island Plot Summary, "Pass the Vegetables, Please." www.imdb.com/title/tt0900567/plotsummary

Kellogg's. "Our Vision & Purpose." www.kelloggs. com/en-in/who-we-are/our-vision-and-purpose. html

King, Jr, Martin. "Martin Luther King – I Have a Dream – Speech – August 28, 1963." www.youtube. com/watch?v=smEqnnklfYs

National Aeronautics and Space Administration, The (NASA). *Artemis I.* www.nasa.gov/mission/artemis-i

Netflix. "About." https://about.netflix.com/en

Niblick, Jay. *What's Your Genius: How the best think for success in the new economy.* St James Books, 2009.

Patagonia. "Our Core Values." www.patagonia.com/core-values

Reidy, Michael J. "Culture Eats Strategy for Breakfast...and what to do about it." Interaction Associates. www.interactionassociates.com/resources/blog/culture-strategy

Robbins, Tony. "The Mentors Who Coached Me: How to Tap into the Power of Multiple Models and Guides to Become Your Best Self." www.tonyrobbins.com/mind-meaning/the-mentors-who-coached-me

Schooley, Skye. "How to Handle a Bad Hire." Business.com, March 23, 2023. www.business.com/articles/cost-of-a-bad-hire

Siocon, Gem. "A Practical Guide to Candidate NPS." AIHR.com, August 24, 2022. www.aihr.com/blog/candidate-nps

Shrayber, Mark. "Costco and 7 Other Popular Companies That Don't Waste Money on Advertising." GoBankingRates.com, October 11, 2021. www.gobankingrates.com/money/business/popular-companies-dont-waste-money-advertising

Sinek, Simon. *Start with Why: How great leaders inspire everyone to take action.* Portfolio, 2011.

TED. "Our mission: Spread ideas, foster community and create impact." www.ted.com/about/our-organization

Thier, Jane. "Most new hires start job searching again within three months, survey finds." *Fortune*, May 4, 2022. https://fortune.com/2022/05/04/new-hires-start-job-searching-again-within-three-months

World Health Organization. "Vision statement by WHO Director-General." www.who.int/director-general/vision

Zappos. "About Us.' www.zappos.com/c/about

Zappos. *Culture Book*. Zappos, 2009.

Zetlin, Minda. "7 Leadership Lessons From the Coach Who Mentored Steve Jobs, Eric Schmidt, and Jeff Bezos." *Inc. Magazine*, April 19, 2016. www.inc.com/minda-zetlin/7-leadership-lessons-from-the-coach-who-mentored-steve-jobs-eric-schmidt-and-jef.html

Acknowledgements

I have so many people to thank for making this book possible, but I want to call out a few amazing humans in particular.

Thank you to Lucy, Joe, Helen, and Jack at Rethink Press for your guidance, your expertise, and your calm through the storm of producing a book. I have counted on your counsel, your professionalism, and your encouragement throughout this process.

Thank you to every client—those I have referenced in the book, and those who continue to inspire me through our work together—for the honor of being part of your growth journey.

Thank you to Natalie Benamou, Wayne Brown, Angela Howard, Aimee Therrian, and Christine Asack for your invaluable feedback on the early draft of this book. Your thoughtful perspectives and suggestions made the book so much better and helped to bring the final version to life.

Thank you to Scott Christopher for agreeing to write the Foreword for this book. You continue to own your walk, contribute your unique voice and gifts, and remind us all that culture and levity matter.

Thank you to Mom and Dad for instilling in me a love of books, of writing, and of teaching others through my own unique craft. You continue to set the example of what a fulfilling life, a committed marriage, and a loving partnership look like.

And thank you to Kevin. You are my husband, my partner, my best friend, and my companion through life. You are my business sounding board and my most vocal advocate. And you are the reason I smile every day. (Well… you and our chinchilla, Munch. You both bring me boundless joy.)

Other Books by Claire Chandler

The Decision Dashboard: Run Your Business from ONE Sheet of Paper

The Whirlpool Effect: Inspire the Flow that Boosts Company Performance

Turning New Leaders into Performance Accelerators: A Guide for Savvy Human Resources and Talent Management Leaders Who Want to Break the "Plug and Pray" Cycle

Leading Beyond a Crisis: A Conversation About What's Next (co-authored with Ben Baker)

Remarkable People Volume 1: How They Overcame Adversity, Achieved Success, & You Can Too! (contributing author)

The Author

President and founder of Talent Boost, Claire Chandler deeply believes that leaders shape culture, and culture drives success. She specializes in helping businesses expand without losing their best talent. Leveraging thirty years of experience in people leadership, human resources, and business ownership, Claire helps leadership teams work together more effectively and efficiently, with less cultural resistance, to accelerate business growth.

Claire's services include keynote and motivational speaking, cultural integration and strategic alignment, thought partnership, talent ecosystems, leadership retreat facilitation, performance acceleration, executive and cohort coaching, organizational assessment and design, team dynamics and alignment, and growth readiness. Her clients often refer to her as their "leadership therapist."

Claire holds a certificate in strategic HR leadership from Cornell's School of Industrial and Labor Relations, a master's degree from the New Jersey Institute of Technology, and a bachelor's degree from Fairfield University. She has appeared as a guest on more than 150 podcasts, is the author of several books on leadership and business strategy, and is a contributing writer for *Forbes*. Her company received the 2023 Best of America Small Business Award as Best Entrepreneur—Business Consulting.

⊕ www.clairechandler.net

⊕ www.talentboost.net

▦ www.linkedin.com/in/clairechandlersphr